ASP.NET Core 2 Fundamentals

Build cross-platform apps and dynamic web services with this server-side web application framework

Onur Gumus
Mugilan T. S. Ragupathi

BIRMINGHAM - MUMBAI

ASP.NET Core 2 Fundamentals

Acquisitions Editor: Koushik Sen
Content Development Editors: Edwin Moses, Rutuja Yerunkar
Production Coordinator: Ratan Pote

First published: August 2018

Production reference: 1300818

Published by Packt Publishing Ltd.
Livery Place
35 Livery Street
Birmingham
B3 2PB, UK.

ISBN 978-1-78953-891-5

www.packtpub.com

`mapt.io`

Mapt is an online digital library that gives you full access to over 5,000 books and videos, as well as industry leading tools to help you plan your personal development and advance your career. For more information, please visit our website.

Why subscribe?

- Spend less time learning and more time coding with practical eBooks and Videos from over 4,000 industry professionals
- Improve your learning with Skill Plans built especially for you
- Get a free eBook or video every month
- Mapt is fully searchable
- Copy and paste, print, and bookmark content

PacktPub.com

Did you know that Packt offers eBook versions of every book published, with PDF and ePub files available? You can upgrade to the eBook version at `www.PacktPub.com` and as a print book customer, you are entitled to a discount on the eBook copy. Get in touch with us at `service@packtpub.com` for more details.

At `www.PacktPub.com`, you can also read a collection of free technical articles, sign up for a range of free newsletters, and receive exclusive discounts and offers on Packt books and eBooks.

Contributors

About the authors

Onur Gumus works as a lead software engineer in Dubai UAE. He has 15 years of experience in .NET and web development. He is a functional programming enthusiast and has completed many large projects with ASP.NET.

Mugilan T. S. Ragupathi has been working on building web-based applications using Microsoft technology for more than a decade. He is active in the ASP.NET community and is running a successful blog, "dotnetodyssey.com", to help his fellow .NET developers. His free beginners' course for ASP.NET MVC 5 at the above blog was well received and is referred to as a concrete reference for beginners. He has also written two free micro e-books, *The 7 Most Popular Recipes of jQuery with ASP.NET Web Forms* and *Value & Reference types in C#*. His books have received a good response.

He can be seen on csharp subreddit/Stack Overflow and is also an active contributor to the ASP.NET community on Quora, going by the username "Mugil-Ragu". He likes to help readers with queries regarding ASP.NET.

Packt is searching for authors like you

If you're interested in becoming an author for Packt, please visit `authors.packtpub.com` and apply today. We have worked with thousands of developers and tech professionals, just like you, to help them share their insight with the global tech community. You can make a general application, apply for a specific hot topic that we are recruiting an author for, or submit your own idea.

Table of Contents

Preface

The book sets the stage with an introduction to web applications and helps you to build an understanding of the tried-and-true MVC architecture. You learn all about views, from what is the Razor view engine to tagging helpers. You gain insight into what models are, how to bind them, and how to migrate databases using the correct model. As you get comfortable in the world of ASP.NET, you learn about validation and routing. You also learn advanced concepts, such as designing a RESTful application, creating entities for it, and creating EF context and migrations.

This book balances theory and exercises, and contains multiple open-ended activities that use real-life business scenarios for you to practice and apply your newly acquired skills in a highly relevant context. We have included over 60 practical activities and exercises across 38 topics to reinforce your learning. By the time you are done reading the book, you will be able to optimally use ASP.NET to develop, unit test, and deploy applications like a pro.

Who this book is for

If you are looking to build web applications using ASP.NET Core or you want to become a pro in building web applications using the Microsoft technology, this is the ideal book for you. Prior exposure and understanding of C#, JavaScript, HTML, and CSS syntax is assumed. This book is written at the time of .NET Core 2.0 preview.

What this book covers

Chapter 1, *Setting the Stage*, begins with explaining the fundamental concepts about web applications—HTTP, client side, and server side. It also discusses the three programming models of ASP.NET MVC. Finally, it provides simple and easy-to-follow step-by-step instructions to set up an ASP.NET Core Web Application project and project structure.

Chapter 2, *Controllers*, explains the role of the controller in ASP.NET MVC applications. It also details the procedure of creating a controller and action methods. It also describes how to make modifications to the controller, such that it uses the view. Finally, it describes how to add a model and pass that model data to your view.

Chapter 3, *Views*, is more hands-on in nature as it teaches how to program in the Razor view engine and use different programming constructs. It also explains in depth how to create and call partial views, create a view component, and create custom Tag Helpers.

Chapter 4, *Models*, explains how models in ASP.NET MVC are used to represent the business domain data. It begins by explaining how to create a simple model and a model specific to ViewModel. It then provides the step-by-step guidance on how to use Entity Framework in ASP.NET MVC applications.

Chapter 5, *Validation*, describes the importance of validating the input data before storing the data for further processing. It begins with a brief explanation of the different types of validation. Moves on to explain how to perform both client-side and server-side validations by using an example. Finally, it covers how to use jQuery libraries to perform unobtrusive JavaScript validation.

Chapter 6, *Routing*, discusses routing along with several options available for customizing it in ASP.NET. Firstly, it teaches how to configure routing using MapRoute. It then, through examples, teaches how to work with different types of routing.

Chapter 7, *Rest Buy*, details the development of a simple shopping cart application called Rest Buy. As with how most projects begin, it discusses the design of Rest Buy. Then, it moves on to discuss the entities for the application. Finally, it deals with EF context and migrations.

Chapter 8, *Adding Features, Testing, and Deployment*, is built around adding the registration feature to our application and testing and deploying it to the cloud. It, therefore, deals with writing unit tests and upgrading it to Bootstrap 4. It also details how to deploy our application to Azure.

To get the most out of this book

You need to have a computer system equipped with the following hardware and software:

- For an optimal experience, we recommend the following hardware configuration:
  - Processor: 3.2 GHz or faster processor (Dual core with multi-threading)
  - Memory: 4 GB of RAM (1.5 GB if running on a virtual machine)
  - Storage: Installations require 20-50 GB of free Hard disk space (depending on features installed the requirement can go up to 130 GB of available space)

- You must also install in advance the following software:
  - Operating System: Windows Server 2008 R2 SP1 (and above) or Windows 7 SP1 (and above)
  - Visual Studio Community 2017 IDE (https://www.visualstudio.com/downloads/)
  - Packages and frameworks, such as NuGet, Bootstrap, and project.json
  - Fiddler (https://www.telerik.com/download/fiddler)

Download the example code files

You can download the example code files for this book from your account at www.packtpub.com. If you purchased this book elsewhere, you can visit www.packtpub.com/support and register to have the files emailed directly to you.

You can download the code files by following these steps:

1. Log in or register at www.packtpub.com.
2. Select the **SUPPORT** tab.
3. Click on **Code Downloads & Errata**.
4. Enter the name of the book in the **Search** box and follow the onscreen instructions.

Once the file is downloaded, please make sure that you unzip or extract the folder using the latest version of:

- WinRAR/7-Zip for Windows
- Zipeg/iZip/UnRarX for Mac
- 7-Zip/PeaZip for Linux

The code bundle for the book is also hosted on GitHub at https://github.com/TrainingByPackt/Beginning-ASP_DOT_NET. In case there's an update to the code, it will be updated on the existing GitHub repository.

We also have other code bundles from our rich catalog of books and videos available at https://github.com/PacktPublishing/. Check them out!

Conventions used

There are a number of text conventions used throughout this book.

CodeInText: Indicates code words in text, database table names, folder names, filenames, file extensions, pathnames, dummy URLs, user input, and Twitter handles. Here is an example: "Mount the downloaded WebStorm-10*.dmg disk image file as another disk in your system."

A block of code is set as follows:

```
public class ValuesController : Controller
{
  // GET api/<controller>
  public IEnumerable<string> Get()
  {
    return new string[] { "value1", "value2" };
  }
}
```

When we wish to draw your attention to a particular part of a code block, the relevant lines or items are set in bold:

```
[default]
exten => s,1,Dial(Zap/1|30)
exten => s,2,Voicemail(u100)
exten => s,102,Voicemail(b100)
exten => i,1,Voicemail(s0)
```

Bold: Indicates a new term, an important word, or words that you see onscreen. For example, words in menus or dialog boxes appear in the text like this. Here is an example: "Open up **Visual Studio 2017**. Navigate to **File | New Project | Web**."

 Warnings or important notes appear like this.

Get in touch

Feedback from our readers is always welcome.

General feedback: Email `feedback@packtpub.com` and mention the book title in the subject of your message. If you have questions about any aspect of this book, please email us at `questions@packtpub.com`.

Errata: Although we have taken every care to ensure the accuracy of our content, mistakes do happen. If you have found a mistake in this book, we would be grateful if you would report this to us. Please visit `www.packtpub.com/submit-errata`, selecting your book, clicking on the Errata Submission Form link, and entering the details.

Piracy: If you come across any illegal copies of our works in any form on the Internet, we would be grateful if you would provide us with the location address or website name. Please contact us at `copyright@packtpub.com` with a link to the material.

If you are interested in becoming an author: If there is a topic that you have expertise in and you are interested in either writing or contributing to a book, please visit `authors.packtpub.com`.

Reviews

Please leave a review. Once you have read and used this book, why not leave a review on the site that you purchased it from? Potential readers can then see and use your unbiased opinion to make purchase decisions, we at Packt can understand what you think about our products, and our authors can see your feedback on their book. Thank you!

For more information about Packt, please visit `packtpub.com`.

1
Setting the Stage

ASP.NET Core—the redesign of ASP.NET from Microsoft—is the server-side web application development framework which helps you to build web applications effectively. This runs on top of the .NET Core platform, which enables your application to be run on a wide variety of platforms, including Linux and macOS. This opens up heaps of opportunities and it is exciting to be a .NET developer in these times.

By the end of this chapter, you will be able to:

- Explain the fundamental concepts about web applications—HTTP, client side, and server side
- Explain the three programming models of ASP.NET MVC
- Get to grips with the philosophy of ASP.NET MVC
- Create your first ASP.NET Core Web Application project and project structure

Introduction to Web Applications

Before discussing the ASP.NET Core and its features, let us understand the fundamentals of web application development.

 Remember this principle: If you want to be an expert at something, you need to be very good at the fundamentals.

How Web Applications Work

All web applications, irrespective of whether they are built using ASP.NET MVC (**MVC** stands for **Model-View-Controller**), which is actually inspired by the success of Ruby on Rails, or any other new shiny technology, work on the HTTP protocol. Some applications use HTTPS (a secure version of HTTP), where data is encrypted before passing through the wire. But HTTPS still uses HTTP.

Symmetric encryption is the conventional method to ensure the integrity of the data transferred. It makes use of only one secret key, called a **symmetric key**, for both encryption and decryption. Both the sender and receiver possess this key. The sender uses it for encryption, while the receiver uses it for decryption. Caesar's Cipher is a good example of symmetric encryption.

Asymmetric encryption makes use of two cryptographic keys. These keys are known as public and private keys. The information to be sent is encrypted by the public key. The private key is used to decrypt the information received. The same algorithm is behind both of these processes. The RSA algorithm is a popular algorithm used in asymmetric encryption.

Encryption ensures the integrity of the data transferred by making use of cryptographic keys. These keys are known only by the sender and the receiver of the data being transferred. This means that the data won't be tampered by anyone else. This prevents man-in-the-middle attacks.

What is the HTTP Protocol?

A protocol is nothing but a set of rules that govern communication. The HTTP protocol is a stateless protocol that follows the request-response pattern.

HTTP stands for **HyperText Transfer Protocol** and is an application protocol which is designed for distributed hypermedia systems. *HyperText* in HyperText Transfer Protocol refers to the structured text that uses hyperlinks for traversing between the documents. Standards for HTTP were developed by the **Internet Engineering Task Force (IETF)** and the **World Wide Web Consortium (W3C)**. The current version of HTTP is HTTP/2 and was standardized in 2015. It is supported by the majority of web browsers, such as Microsoft Edge, Google Chrome, and Mozilla Firefox.

HTTP/2's Edge over HTTP/1.x

At a high level, HTTP/2:

- Is binary, instead of textual
- Is fully multiplexed, instead of ordered and blocking
- Uses one connection for parallelism
- Uses header compression to reduce overhead
- Allows servers to push responses proactively into client caches

Request-Response Pattern

Before talking about the request-response pattern, let's discuss a couple of terms: client and server. A server is a computing resource that receives the requests from the clients and serves them. A server, typically, is a high-powered machine with huge memory to process many requests. A client is a computing resource that sends a request and receives the response. A client could typically be any application that sends the requests.

Coming back to the request-response pattern, when you request a resource from a server, the server responds to you with the requested resource. A resource could be anything—a web page, text file, image, or another data format.

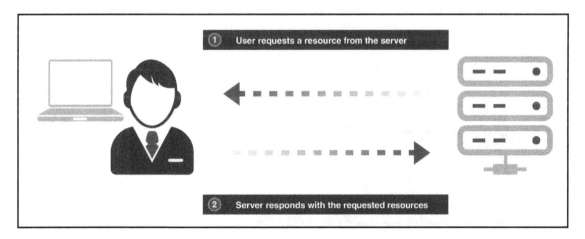

You fire a request. The server responds with the resource. This is called a **request-response pattern**.

Stateless Nature of HTTP

When you request for the same resource again, the server responds to you with the requested resource again without having any knowledge of the fact that the same was requested and served earlier. The HTTP protocol inherently does not have any knowledge of the state of any of the previous requests received and served. There are several mechanisms available that maintain the state, but the HTTP protocol does not maintain the state by itself. We will explain the mechanisms to maintain the state later.

Advantages to HTTP

Here are the few advantages of using HTTP protocol:

- HTTP is a text-based protocol that runs on top of TCP/IP
- HTTP is firewall-friendly
- HTTP is easier to debug since it is text based
- All browsers know about HTTP. Thus, it is extremely portable on any device or any platform
- It standardizes the application-level protocol into a proper request–response cycle

With TCP/IP, everybody has to invent their own application protocol. HTTP is traditionally not full duplex, but with HTML5 we can use Web Sockets to upgrade HTTP connections to a full duplex connection.

Work with the Statelessness and the Request-Response Pattern

With the help of a simple practical example, let's work with the statelessness and the request-response pattern. Here are the steps:

1. Type this URL: `https://en.wikipedia.org/wiki/ASP.NET_Core`. This is a Wikipedia web page about ASP.NET Core.

We'll talk about ASP.NET later in this chapter.

2. From the preceding URL, the browser fires a request to the Wikipedia server.

3. The web server at Wikipedia serves you the ASP.NET Core web page.

4. Your browser receives that web page and presents it.

5. Now, request the same page again by typing the same URL again (`https://en.wikipedia.org/wiki/ASP.NET_Core`) and pressing *Enter*.

6. The browser again fires the request to the Wikipedia server.

7. Wikipedia serves you the same ASP.NET Core web page without being aware of the fact that the same resource was requested previously.

8. Here's a screenshot from the Wikipedia page showing requests and responses:

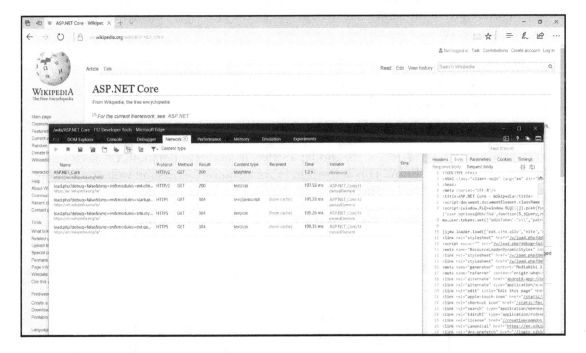

 As mentioned earlier, there are several mechanisms to maintain the state. Let us assume, for the time being, that no such mechanism is implemented here.

Client Side and Server Side

It is necessary to understand the client side and server side of web applications and what can be done on either side. With respect to web applications, your client is the browser and your server could be the web server/application server.

The client side is whatever that happens in your browser. It is the place where your JavaScript code runs and your HTML elements reside.

The server side is whatever happens at the server at the other end of your computer. The request that you fire from your browser has to travel through the wire (probably across the network) to execute some server-side code and return the appropriate response. Your browser is oblivious to the server-side technology or the language your server-side code is written in. The server side is also the place where your C# code resides.

Let us discuss some of the facts to make things clearer:

- **Fact 1**: All browsers can only understand HTML, CSS (Cascading Style Sheets), and JavaScript, irrespective of the browser vendor:
  - You might be using Microsoft Edge, Firefox, Chrome, or any other browser. Still, the fact is that your browser can understand only HTML, CSS, and JavaScript. It cannot understand C#, Java, or Ruby. This is the reason why you can access the web applications built using any technology by the same browser:

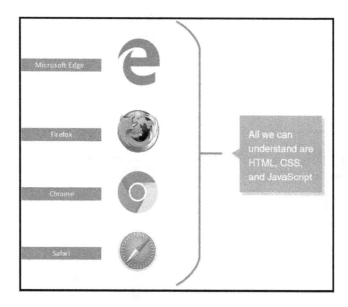

- **Fact 2**: The purpose of any web development framework is to convert your server-side code to HTML, CSS, and JavaScript:
  - This is related to the previous point. As browsers can only understand HTML, CSS, and JavaScript, all the web development technologies should convert your server-side code to HTML, CSS, and JavaScript so that your browser can understand. This is the primary purpose of any web development framework. This is true whether you build your web applications using ASP.NET MVC, ASP.NET Web Forms, Ruby on Rails, or J2EE. Each web development framework may have a unique concept/implementation regarding how to generate the HTML, CSS, and JavaScript, and may handle features such as security performance differently. But still, each framework has to produce the HTML, because that's what your browsers understand.

Programming Styles – RPC versus REST

Basically, there are two common styles when programming HTTP: Remote Procedure Calls and REST. Let's look at each here:

- **Remote Procedure Calls**: In the RPC style, we usually treat HTTP as a transport medium and do not focus on HTTP itself. We are simply piggybacking on HTTP. Our service provides some set of operations that are callable directly. In other words, from our client, we call methods as if we are calling normal methods and passing parameters. Usually, RPC is applied via **SOAP (Simple Object Access Protocol)**, which is another XML protocol that runs on top of HTTP. RPC was popular before 2008, and these days the RESTful approach is more popular, since RPC style introduces more coupling between client and server.
- **REST**: REST stands for Representational State Transfer. In REST, we use URLs to represent our resources, such as `https://api.example.com/books/`. This URL is basically an identifier for a book collection. And for example, the following could be an identifier for the book with ID 1: `https://api.example.com/books/1`.

Then, we use HTTP verbs to interact with these resources. HTTP verbs and HTTP methods are synonyms. The available methods in HTTP are `GET`, `HEAD`, `POST`, `PUT`, `DELETE`, `TRACE`, `OPTIONS`, `CONNECT`, and `PATCH`. So, when we make an HTTP request with `GET`, we are basically asking the web server to return that resource representation. And that representation can change, even for each request.

The server can return XML for one request and JSON for another, depending on what a client accepts, which is specified by the `Accept` header.

Why do we need REST? It is all about standardization. Suppose that we access a resource by using the `GET` verb; we inherently know that we are not altering anything in the server. Similarly, when we send a request via `PUT`, we inherently know that the requests are idempotent, meaning duplicate requests won't change anything to the same resource. Once we have this standard established, our application behaves like a browser. Just like a browser does not need documentation of an API while walking through the pages, our applications will not need documentation, but only adhere to the standards.

Working with HTTP Methods

HTTP defines methods (sometimes referred to as *verbs*) to indicate the desired actions to be performed on the identified resources. It is a part of HTTP specification. Even though all the requests of the HTTP protocol follow the request-response pattern, the way the requests are sent can vary from one to the next. The HTTP method defines how the request is being sent to the server.

The available methods in HTTP are `GET`, `HEAD`, `POST`, `PUT`, `DELETE`, `TRACE`, `OPTIONS`, `CONNECT`, and `PATCH`. In most of the web applications, the `GET` and `POST` methods are widely used. In this section, we will discuss these methods. Later, we will discuss other HTTP methods on a need-to-know basis.

The GET Method

`GET` is a method of the HTTP protocol which is used to get a resource from the server. Requests which use the `GET` method should only retrieve the data and should not have any side effect. This means that if you fire the same `GET` request again and again, you should get the same data, and there should not be any change in the state of the server as a result of this `GET` request.

In the `GET` method, the parameters are sent as part of the request URL and will therefore be visible to the end user. The advantage of this approach is that the user can bookmark the URL and visit the page again whenever they want. An example is `https://yourwebsite.com/?tech=mvc6db=sql`.

We are passing a couple of parameters in the preceding GET request. tech is the first parameter, with the value mvc6, and db is the second parameter, with the value sql. Assume your website takes the preceding parameters with values and searches in your database to retrieve the blog posts that talk about mvc6 and sql before presenting those blog posts to the user:

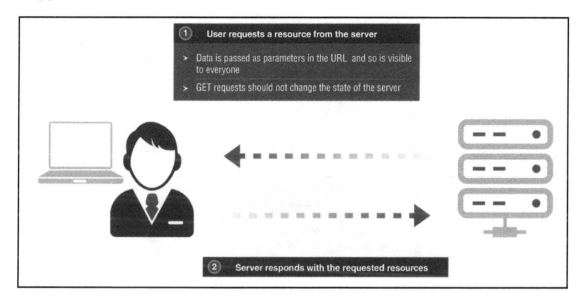

The disadvantage of the GET method is that, as the data is passed in clear text in the URL as parameters, it cannot be used to send sensitive information. Moreover, most browsers have limitations on the number of characters in the URL, so, when using GET requests, we cannot send large amounts of data.

The POST Method

The POST request is generally used to update or create resources at the server, as well as when you want to send some data to be processed by the server. Especially in the context of REST, it is more accurate to consider POST as a process rather than Create.

Data is passed in the body of the request. This has the following implications:

- You can send relatively sensitive information to the server, as the data is embedded in the body of the request and it will not be visible to the end user in the URL. However, note that your data is never truly secure unless you use HTTPS. Even if you send the data within the request body, without HTTPS, it is very easy for someone in the middle to eavesdrop on your data.
- As the data is not sent through the request URL, it does not take up space in the URL, and it therefore has no issues with the URL length limitations:

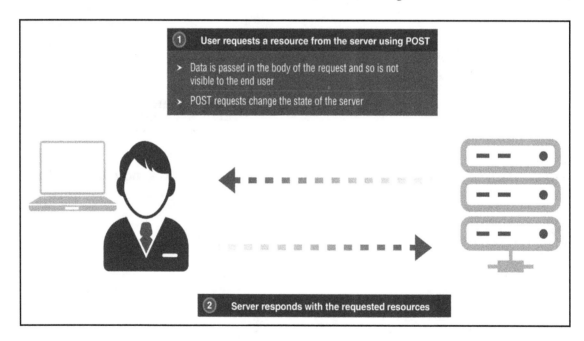

As we have covered the fundamentals, we can now proceed to discuss ASP.NET.

List of Important Methods

Before we discuss the HTTP methods, let's review three aspects of HTTP verbs:

- **Idempotency**: Idempotency is an important concept in HTTP calls. In idempotent requests, you can change the server-side state (however, only once). That is, if you make multiple idempotent requests to the server, the net effect will be as if you have done one request.

- **Safety**: Safe requests simply do not cause any side effects. They are only used to retrieve data. By side effects, we refer to any persistent changes in memory or database or any other external system. Registering a user is a side effect. Making a money transfer is a side effect. But viewing user information is not a side effect.

- **Cacheablity**: Server or client or proxies can cache the responses for the requests.

The following table lists the important HTTP methods and their aspects:

Method	Description	Idempotent	Safe	Cacheable
GET	Reads a resource.	Yes	Yes	Yes
POST	Creates a resource or triggers a process.	No	No	No
PUT	Puts something onto a resource ID. Overrides if something exits. Not to be confused with an update.	Yes	No	No
PATCH	Updates a part of a resource.	No	No	No
DELETE	Removes a resource.	Yes	No	No

In the preceding table, we can see that the GET method is the only safe method. And that's why, for example, search engines like Google only use GET methods to scan our side. Adhering to this standard makes sure nothing is changed during a search engine scan.

Other Methods

Some of the other notable methods are as follows:

- CONNECT: This is used for HTTP tunneling for security reasons. It's not common in typical web applications and services.
- TRACE: It is used for debugging purposes. It's not common in typical web applications and services.
- OPTIONS: By using the OPTIONS verb, we can query which methods are supported by the web server for that resource.

Here's some part of the response after the OPTIONS method is invoked:

```
HTTP/1.1 200 OK
Allow: OPTIONS, GET, HEAD, POST
```

Activity: Working with the Request-Response Pattern

Scenario

Your company wants you to monitor the network traffic of their website. Here, we use https://www.google.com/ as a reference.

Aim

To check the request-response pattern for https://www.google.com/.

Steps for completion

1. Open your favorite browser.
2. Hit *F12* to open developer tools.
3. Then, click on the **Network** tab.
4. Next, go to https://www.google.com/.
5. Study the header body for request and response.

You should see something similar to what is shown in the following screenshot:

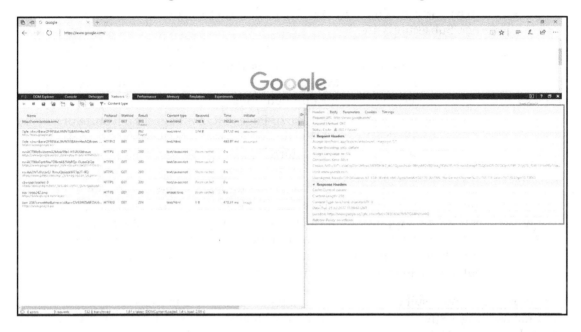

Introduction to ASP.NET

ASP.NET is a server-side web application development framework, developed by Microsoft, allowing developers to build web applications, websites, and web services.

It is currently fully open source in this URL and is still maintained by Microsoft: `https:// github.com/aspnet`

Basically, ASP.NET has three main programming models: ASP.NET Web Forms, ASP.NET MVC, and ASP.NET Web Pages. They form part of the ASP.NET Framework in this manner:

- **ASP.NET for .NET Framework**: This has the following sub sections:
  - **Web Forms**: This is known for rapid application development. This tries to mimic desktop behavior.
  - **MVC**: This applies the Model-View-Controller pattern.
  - **Web API**: This is an MVC-style web service.
  - **Single-Page Application**: Here, the server gives the initial HTML request, but further rendering happens entirely within the

browser.

- **ASP.NET Core**: It is the new ASP.NET Platform that runs in a cross-platform manner. Subsections are:
    - **Web API**: This is primarily used for developing web services.
    - **Web Application**: This is used for MVC Applications. It can be used for developing web services too. Web API and MVC have become an almost unified thing.
    - **Web Application** (Razor Pages): Razor Pages is a feature of ASP.NET Core MVC that makes coding page-focused scenarios easier and more productive.

A recent trend for developers is the use of Single-Page Application frameworks on top of web services like Web APIs. However, MVC and Single-Page Application frameworks also play nicely together. In the future, we expect Microsoft to put more effort on .NET Core instead of .NET Framework. .NET Framework is already mature. Perhaps it will be put into maintenance mode but nothing is certain yet.

Even though the end result of all of the preceding programming models is to produce dynamic web pages effectively, the methodologies that they follow differ from each other. Let us discuss ASP.NET MVC.

ASP.NET MVC

ASP.NET MVC is the implementation of the MVC pattern in ASP.NET. The disadvantages of ASP.NET Web Forms which tried to mimic Windows development in the web environment, such as limited control over the generation of HTML, coupling with business code and UI code, hard-to-grasp, and complex page life cycle, are resolved in ASP.NET MVC. As most of the modern applications are controlled by client-side JavaScript libraries/frameworks, such as **jQuery**, **KnockoutJS**, **AngularJS**, and **ReactJS**, having complete control over the generated HTML is of paramount importance. As for Knockout, Angular, and React, these single-page libraries actually generate the HTML directly within the browser via their own template engines. In other words, the rendering is done in the browser rather than the server. This frees up server resources and it allows the web application to behave just like a disconnected application, as in mobile apps.

Let us talk a bit about the Model-View-Controller pattern and how it benefits the web application development.

The Model-View-Controller Pattern

This is a software architectural pattern which helps in defining the responsibility for each of the components and how they fit together in achieving the overall goal. This pattern is primarily used in building user interfaces and is applicable in many areas, including developing desktop applications and web applications. But I am going to explain the MVC pattern from the context of web development.

Primarily, the MVC pattern has three components:

- **Model**: This component represents your domain data. Note that this is not your database. This model component can talk to your database, but the model only represents your domain data. For example, if you are building an e-commerce web application, the model component may contain classes such as `Product`, `Supplier`, and `Inventory`.
- **View**: This component is responsible for what to present to the user. Usually, this component would contain your HTML and CSS files. This may also include the layout information governing how your web application looks to the end user.
- **Controller**: As the name implies, the controller is responsible for interacting with different components. It receives the request (through the routing module), talks to the model, and sends the appropriate view to the user.

The following image speaks of the MVC pattern:

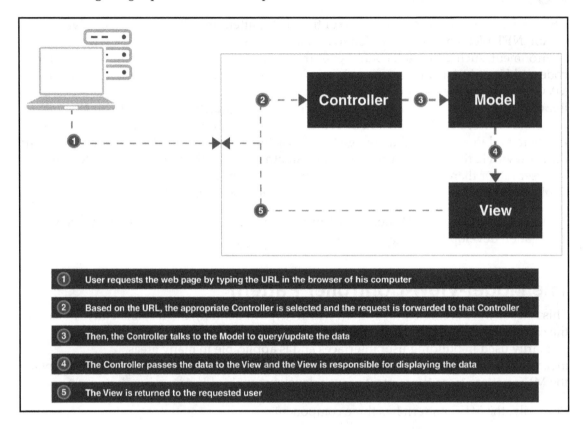

This separation of responsibilities brings great flexibility to the web application development, allowing each area to be managed separately and independently.

The Code for ASP.NET Core is as follows:

```
public class ValuesController : Controller
{
// GET api/<controller>
public IEnumerable<string> Get()
{
return new string[] { "value1", "value2" };
}
}
```

Basically, each controller is represented by a class derived from the `Controller` class, although we can also write controllers without deriving from `Controller`. Each public method of the controller represents actions.

In this case, if we define a `GET` method (accessed via `www.yoursite.com/controller` without writing `GET`), it returns a string array as a response. How these strings are returned depends on the content negotiation.

A File-Based Project

Whenever you add a file or folder in your file system (inside the ASP.NET Core project folder), the changes will automatically be reflected in your application.

We bundle our static files into one file because for each static file, a browser will make a separate request to the server to retrieve it. If you have 100 CSS and JavaScript files, this means there will be 100 separate requests to retrieve those files. Obviously, reducing the number of requests will certainly improve the performance of your application. Thus, bundling is effectively decreasing the number of requests.

HTTP/2 uses only 1 persistent connection for all files and requests. Thus, bundling is less useful in HTTP/2. However, it's still recommended since HTTP/1.x is here to stay for a long time.
The development and deployment of an ASP.NET Core application on a Linux machine will be explained in a later chapter.

These are the important folders and files in a file-based project:

Folder/File	Description
Controllers	This folder contains all of your controller files. Controllers are responsible for handling requests, communicating models, and generating the views.
Models	All of your classes representing domain data will be present in this folder.
Views	These are files that contain your frontend components and are presented to the end users of the application. This folder contains all of your RazorView files.
wwwroot	This folder acts as a root folder and it is the ideal container to place all of your static files, such as CSS and JavaScript files. All the files which are placed in the wwwroot folder can be directly accessed from the path, without going through the controller.
Other files	The appsettings.json file is the configuration file where you can configure application-level settings. Previously, .xml files were used for configuration; however, the .json format is less verbose, and **Bower** and **npm (Node Package Manager)** are client-side technologies, supported by ASP.NET Core applications. The Bundle.config file allows us to configure how to bundle our CSS and JS files into one file.

Here's the project structure of ASP.NET Core:

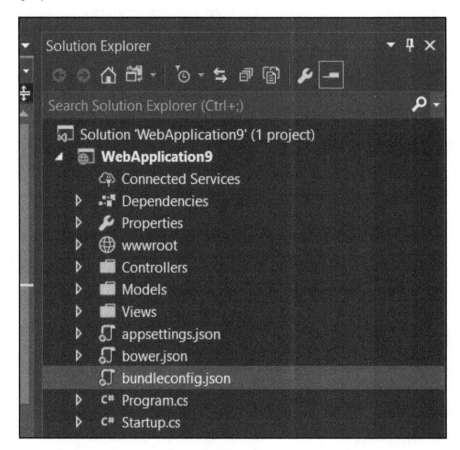

Despite the fact that current ASP.NET Core templates are using Bower, Bower itself is obsolete now. Instead, npm or yarn is recommended. Just like NuGet, the JavaScript world needed package managers as there are hundreds of thousands of libraries and they have complex dependencies on each other. These package managers allow you to automate the installation and upgrades of these libraries by writing single commands from the command line.

Creating Your First Project

Follow this steps to create your first project:

1. Open up Visual Studio 2017. Navigate to **File** | **New Project** | **Web**. You'll be presented with this screen:

2. Select **ASP.NET Core Web Application**. Optionally, give a name to your project, or accept the default. Then, click on **OK**.
3. Make sure you select **.NET Core 2.0**. If it doesn't show up, download .NET Core SDK from `https://www.microsoft.com/net/download/` core and restart Visual Studio. Then select **Web Application** and click on **OK**.
4. Right-click on your project and click on **Build**. This will restore the dependencies.

Creating Your First Application

It is now time to create your first ASP.NET Core application.

Fire up Visual Studio and follow these steps:

1. Create a project by selecting **File | New Project** in Visual Studio. The first option is for creating an earlier version of the ASP.NET web application. The second option is for creating the ASP.NET Core application using the .NET Core framework. NET Core supports only the core functionalities. The advantage of using the .NET core library is that it can be deployed on any platform. Select **ASP.NET Core Web Application**:

Routing and controllers work together to render the correct view.

We'll use the name `Lesson2` here to avoid reinventing the wheel in `Chapter 2`, *Controllers*.

2. Select the **Empty** template from the list of ASP.NET Core templates. The second option is for creating the Web API application (for building the HTTP-based services) and the third option is for creating a web application containing some basic functionalities which you can run out of the box, without you ever needing to write anything:

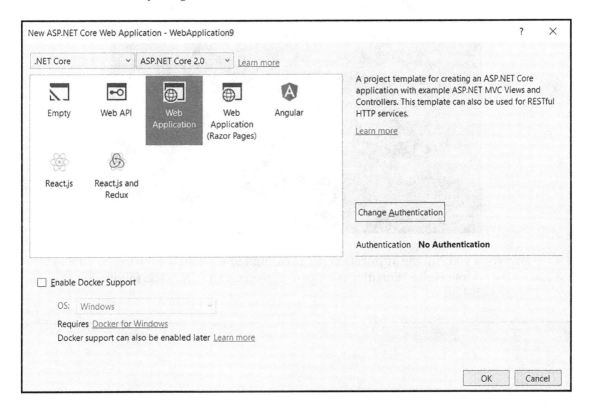

3. Once you click on **OK** in the window, as shown in the preceding screenshot (after selecting the **Empty** template option), a solution will be created, as shown in the following screenshot:

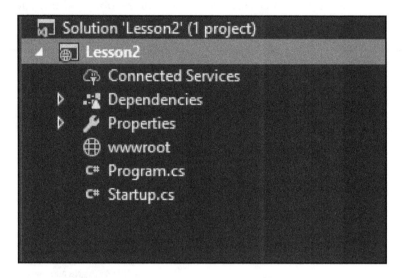

4. When you run the application (by pressing *F5*) without any changes, you'll get the simple **Hello World!** text on your screen, as shown in the following screenshot:

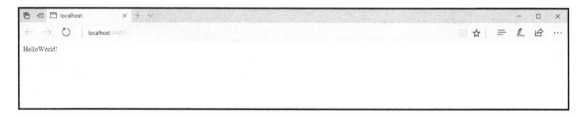

We have not done any coding in this newly created application. So, have you thought about how it displays the text **Hello World!**?

The answer lies in the `Startup.cs` file, which contains a class by the name of Startup.

When an exception occurs, we want to display the callstack for better diagnosis, for instance. However, doing so in a production environment would be a security risk. Hence, we have development-specific code.

ASP.NET Core runtime calls the `ConfigureServices` and `Configure` methods through the main method. For example, if you want to configure any service, you can add it here. Any custom configuration for your application can be added to this `Configure` method:

```
public void ConfigureServices(IServiceCollection services)
{
}
public void Configure(IApplicationBuilder app, IHostingEnvironment
env)
{
  if (env.IsDevelopment())
  {
    app.UseDeveloperExceptionPage();
  }
  app.Run(async (context) =>
  {
    await context.Response.WriteAsync("Hello World!");
  });
}
```

There are only a couple of statements in the Configure method. Let us leave aside `async`, `await`, and `context` for the moment in the second statement, which we will discuss later. In essence, the second statement tells the runtime to return **Hello World!** for all the incoming requests, irrespective of the incoming URL.

When you type the URL `http://localhost:50140/Hello` in your browser, it will still return the same **Hello World!**

This is the reason we got the **Hello World!** when we ran the application.

As we have chosen the **Empty** template while creating the ASP.NET Core application, no component will have been installed. Even MVC won't be installed by default when you select the **Empty** template as we did.

Summary

In this chapter, you've learned the basics of web development, including what constitutes the server side and client side. HTTP is a key protocol in web development. We have even discussed the features of ASP.NET Core. We've looked at REST and RPC as two web programming styles.

We have also discussed the new project structure of the ASP.NET Core application and the changes when compared to the previous versions.

In the next chapter, we are going to discuss the controllers and their roles and functionalities. We'll also build a controller and associated action methods and see how they work.

2
Controllers

In the previous chapter, we discussed that all web applications receive requests from the server and produce a response that is delivered back to the end user. This chapter covers the role of controllers in ASP.NET MVC applications and details the procedure of creating a controller and action methods.

By the end of this chapter, you will be able to:

- Explain the role of the controller in ASP.NET MVC applications
- Work with the routing engine
- Install the ASP.NET Core NuGet packages in your application
- Create your first controller and action methods
- Add a view and make the changes that allow your controller to use that view
- Add a model and pass that model data to your view

Role of the Controller in ASP.NET MVC Applications

A controller does the job of receiving the request and producing the output based on the input data in ASP.NET MVC. You can imagine controllers as the entrance point to your business flow that organizes the application flow.

 If you are intending to write a complex application, it is best to avoid business logic in your controllers. Instead, your controllers should call your business logic. In this way, you can keep the core part of your business technology-agnostic.

At the high level, the controller orchestrates between the model and the view, and sends the output back to the user. This is also the place where authentication is usually done through action filters. Action filters are basically interceptors and will be discussed in detail in the *Filters* section of this chapter. The following diagram illustrates the high-level flow of a request (with the steps) in ASP.NET MVC and shows us how the controller fits into the big picture:

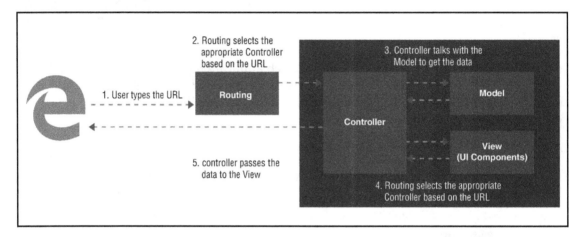

The following is the sequence of events that will happen at the high level when the user is accessing the ASP.NET Core application:

1. The user types the URL in the browser.
2. Based on the pattern of the URL, the routing engine selects the appropriate controller.
3. The controller talks to the model to get any relevant data through its action methods. Action methods are methods within a controller class.
4. The controller then passes the data to the view to present it in a viewable format, typically as HTML elements.
5. The view is finally delivered to the user, which he would be viewing in his browser.

Before discussing the controller, let us discuss the fundamentals of routing concepts, as the routing engine only chooses the appropriate `controller` and `action` method at runtime.

Ideal Flow of Data for a Layered Web Application

Let's see what an ideal flow of data for a layered web application looks like. Have a look at the following diagram:

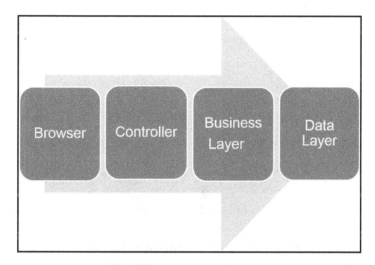

Let's analyze the diagram. Here's the explanation:

- The **Browser** is the medium through which the user types the URL
- The appropriate **Controller** gets into action
- The **Controller** communicates with the **Business Layer** and the **Data Layer**
- The **Business Layer** returns the data requested by the user to the **Controller**

The business and the data layers constitute the model part of the MVC. Now, what are these layers? The business layer's job is to put the business logic or functionality to use. The data layer concerns with external systems such as databases. It provides access to these systems.

Introduction to Routing

The routing engine is responsible for getting the incoming request and routing that request to the appropriate controller based on the URL pattern. We can configure the routing engine so that it can choose the appropriate controller based on the relevant information. In other words, routing is a programmatic mapping that states which method of which controller is to be invoked based on some URL pattern.

By convention, ASP.NET MVC follows this pattern: `Controller/Action/Id`.

If the user types the URL `http://yourwebsite.com/Hello/Greeting/1`, the routing engine selects the `Hello controller` class and `Greeting action` method within the `Hello controller`, and passes the `Id` value as `1`. `XXXController` is a naming convention and it is assumed your controllers are always ending with a controller suffix. You can give default values to some of the parameters and make some of the parameters optional.

The following is the sample configuration:

```
The template: "{controller=Hello}/{action=Greeting}/{id?}");
```

In the preceding configuration, we are giving three instructions to the routing engine:

- Use the routing pattern `controller/action/id`.
- Use the default values `Hello` and `Greeting` for `controller` and `action` respectively, if the values for `controller` or `action` are not supplied in the URL.
- Make the `id` parameter optional so that the URL does not need to have this information. If the URL contains this Id information, it will use it. Otherwise, the id information will not be passed to the `action` method.

Let us discuss how the routing engine selects the `controller` classes, `action` methods, and `id` values for different URLs. We'll start with `URL1`, here:

```
URL1: http://localhost/
Controller: Hello
Action method: Greeting
Id: no value is passed for the id parameter
```

The `Hello` controller is passed as the default value as per the routing configuration, as no value is passed as the controller in the URL.

The following `action` method will be picked up by the routing handler when the preceding URL is passed:

```
public class HelloController : Controller
{
  public ActionResult Greeting(int id)
  {
    return View();
  }
}
```

Let's look at URL2, here:

```
URL2: http://localhost/Hello/Greeting2
Controller: Hello
Action method: Greeting2
Id: no value is passed for the id parameter
```

 The Hello controller will be chosen as the URL contains Hello as the first parameter, and the Greeting2 action method will be chosen as the URL contains Greeting2 as the second parameter. Please note that the default value mentioned in the configuration would be picked only when no value is present in the URL. As the id parameter is optional and the URL does not contain the value for id, no value is passed to the id parameter.

The following action method Greeting2 will be picked up by the routing handler when the preceding URL is passed:

```
public class HelloController : Controller
{
  public ActionResult Greeting(int id)
  {
    return View();
  }
  public ActionResult Greeting2(int id)
  {
      return View();
  }
}
```

Let's look at URL3, here:

```
URL3: http://localhost/Hello2/Greeting2
Controller: Hello2
Action method: Greeting2
Id: no value is passed for the id parameter
```

 As Hello2 is passed as the first parameter, the Hello2 controller will be selected, and Greeting2 is the action method selected since Greeting2 is passed as the second parameter. As the id parameter is optional and no value is passed for the parameter id, no value will be passed for the id.

The following action method will be picked up by the routing handler when the preceding URL is passed:

```
public class Hello2Controller : Controller
{
  public ActionResult Greeting2(int id)
  {
    return View();
  }
}
```

Let's look at URL4, here:

```
URL4: http://localhost/Hello3/Greeting2/1
Controller: Hello3
Action method: Greeting2
Id: 1
```

 Hello3 is the controller selected as it is mentioned as the first parameter. Greeting4 is the action method, and 1 is the value passed as the id.

The following action method will be picked up by the routing handler when the preceding URL is passed:

```
public class Hello3Controller : Controller
{
  public ActionResult Greeting2(int id)
  {
    return View();
  }
}
```

Another common pattern is to use more RESTful programming practice. We instead treat URLs as Resource ID and send the action as an HTTP method such as GET or POST.

So, from a classical MVC point of view, if you need to edit a book, you send a post to `http://yourwebsite.com/Books/Edit/1` with a POST request, and the body contains the new book details.

However, from a RESTful standpoint, you would use `http://yourwebsite.com/Books/1` with a PUT or PATCH request, and the request body contains the book details.

The point of RESTful programming is to have some sort of standardization that everyone agrees on at least up to a certain degree. For the RESTful case you don't have to document your API. Everyone knows that a PUT request replaces the resource that is by HTTP standard. However, for the actions, someone can call it Edit whereas another can call it Update. Of course, with web applications that are not intended to be used as an API, this is less valuable. However, you might want a reusable API along with your web application. That's where the RESTful approach shines. For that case, your web pages just become a special case of the API and you have less duplication.

Activity: Finding the Correct Method Invoked for a URL

Scenario

There has been a cyber attack in your company. The administrator wants to know which method has been invoked by the hacker by sending you the malicious URL.

Aim

To find the correct method invoked for the given URL (`http://localhost/Hello3/Welcome/1`).

Steps for completion

Open your editor and type the following code:

 Go to `https://goo.gl/2Jy3W4` to access the code.

```
public class Hello3Controller : Controller
{
    public ActionResult Welcome(int id)
    {
      return View();
    }
    ...
    ...
    {
      return View();
    }
}
```

Once the request reaches the controller, the controller will create a response by talking to the model and may pass the data to the view, and the view will then be rendered to the end user.

 We will discuss routing in detail in a later chapter.

Installing the ASP.NET Core NuGet Package in Your Application

We'll straight away jump to installing the ASP.NET Core NuGet package in your application.

Follow these steps to install the NuGet package of ASP.NET MVC:

1. Right-click on the dependencies, and select the **Manage NuGet Packages** option:

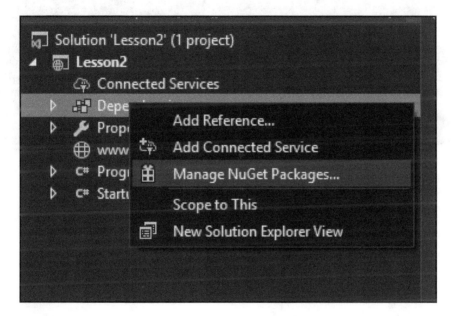

2. We will see that a package called **Microsoft.ASPNetCore.All** is installed (as shown in the following screenshot). This package is actually a meta package that installs most of the dependencies we need.

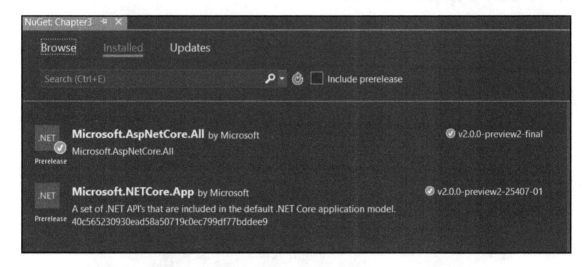

3. If we extend this package from dependencies, we will see:

```
▲  🐹 Microsoft.AspNetCore.All (2.0.0-preview2-final)
   ▷  🐹 Microsoft.AspNetCore (2.0.0-preview2-final)
   ▷  🐹 Microsoft.AspNetCore.Antiforgery (2.0.0-preview2-final)
   ▷  🐹 Microsoft.AspNetCore.ApplicationInsights.HostingStartup (2.0.0-preview
   ▷  🐹 Microsoft.AspNetCore.Authentication (2.0.0-preview2-final)
   ▷  🐹 Microsoft.AspNetCore.Authentication.Abstractions (2.0.0-preview2-fina
   ▷  🐹 Microsoft.AspNetCore.Authentication.Cookies (2.0.0-preview2-final)
   ▷  🐹 Microsoft.AspNetCore.Authentication.Core (2.0.0-preview2-final)
   ▷  🐹 Microsoft.AspNetCore.Authentication.Facebook (2.0.0-preview2-final)
   ▷  🐹 Microsoft.AspNetCore.Authentication.Google (2.0.0-preview2-final)
   ▷  🐹 Microsoft.AspNetCore.Authentication.JwtBearer (2.0.0-preview2-final)
   ▷  🐹 Microsoft.AspNetCore.Authentication.MicrosoftAccount (2.0.0-preview2
   ▷  🐹 Microsoft.AspNetCore.Authentication.OAuth (2.0.0-preview2-final)
   ▷  🐹 Microsoft.AspNetCore.Authentication.OpenIdConnect (2.0.0-preview2-f
   ▷  🐹 Microsoft.AspNetCore.Authentication.Twitter (2.0.0-preview2-final)
   ▷  🐹 Microsoft.AspNetCore.Authorization (2.0.0-preview2-final)
   ▷  🐹 Microsoft.AspNetCore.Authorization.Policy (2.0.0-preview2-final)
   ▷  🐹 Microsoft.AspNetCore.AzureAppServices.HostingStartup (2.0.0-preview
   ▷  🐹 Microsoft.AspNetCore.AzureAppServicesIntegration (2.0.0-preview2-fin
   ▷  🐹 Microsoft.AspNetCore.CookiePolicy (2.0.0-preview2-final)
   ▷  🐹 Microsoft.AspNetCore.Cors (2.0.0-preview2-final)
   ▷  🐹 Microsoft.AspNetCore.Cryptography.Internal (2.0.0-preview2-final)
   ▷  🐹 Microsoft.AspNetCore.Cryptography.KeyDerivation (2.0.0-preview2-fina
   ▷  🐹 Microsoft.AspNetCore.DataProtection (2.0.0-preview2-final)
   ▷  🐹 Microsoft.AspNetCore.DataProtection.Abstractions (2.0.0-preview2-fina
   ▷  🐹 Microsoft.AspNetCore.DataProtection.AzureStorage (2.0.0-preview2-fir
```

So, everything we need is already installed regardless of using an empty project or not.

ASP.NET Core is installed in our application. Now, we need to tell our application to use ASP.NET MVC.

This needs a couple of changes to the `Startup.cs` file:

1. Configure the application to add the MVC service. This can be done by adding the following line to the `ConfigureServices` method of the Startup class:

 Go to `https://goo.gl/RPXUaw` to access the code.

```
public void ConfigureServices(IServiceCollection services)
{
    services.AddMvc();
}
```

2. Configure the routing so that our correct controllers will be picked for the incoming requests based on the URL entered. The following code snippet needs to be updated in the `Configure` method of the `Startup.cs` file:

 Go to `https://goo.gl/Xa1YcD` to access the code.

```
public void Configure(IApplicationBuilder app, IHostingEnvironment
env)
{
    if (env.IsDevelopment())
    {
        app.UseDeveloperExceptionPage();
    }
    app.UseMvc(routes =>
    {
        routes.MapRoute(
        name: "default",
        template: "{controller=Home}
        /{action=Index}/{id?}");
    });
}
```

In the preceding statement, we are configuring the routes for our application.

In this chapter, and most of the chapters in this course, we will write codes manually or choose an **Empty** template instead of relying on scaffolding templates. For those who are new to the term scaffolding, scaffolding is a feature that generates all the necessary boilerplate code for you for the selected item (for example, the controller) instead of you needing to write everything.

 Though scaffolding templates are useful and save time in generating the boilerplate code, they hide many of the details that beginners have to understand. Once you write code manually, you'll know all the intricacies of how each of the components is contributing to the big picture. Once you are strong in the fundamentals, you can use scaffolding templates to save you time in writing the boilerplate code. Scaffolding is also useful for creating quick administrative pages to edit our database.

Our First Controller

Before creating the controller, we need to remove the following app.Run statement as this will return **Hello World!** for all the incoming requests. As we want incoming requests to be handled by the controllers, we need to remove the following code from the Configure method of the Startup class:

```
app.Run(async (context) =>
{
    await context.Response.WriteAsync("Hello World!");
};
```

We have installed ASP.NET Core in our application. So, we are geared up for creating our first ASP.NET Core controller. Create a folder with the name `Controllers` and add a new controller from the context menu, as shown in the following screenshot:

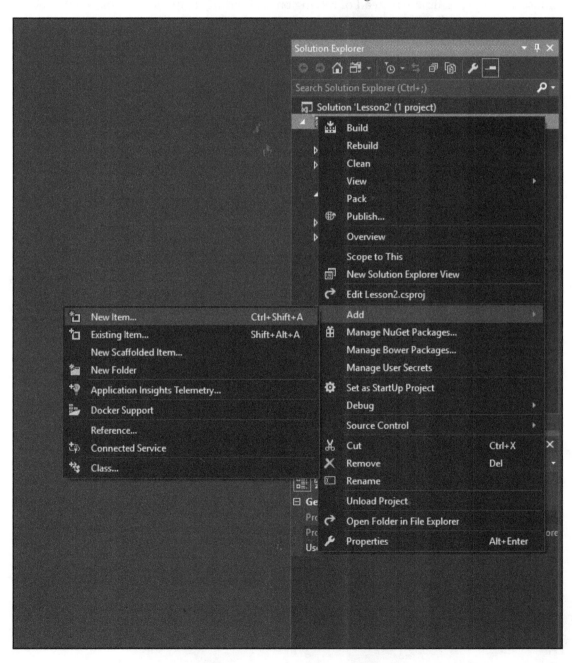

Context basically represents the request-response pair along with other metadata necessary to process the request.

For people who used OWIN to develop your own web custom framework without using MVC, it is analogous to `IOwinContext`. And apparently, `app.Run` would be a good entry point to handle HTTP requests manually or for writing a custom framework. After all, HTTP is about retrieving requests and returning responses.

Once you navigate to **Add** | **New Item**, you will be shown the following list of options. We are going to add an MVC controller class to our project:

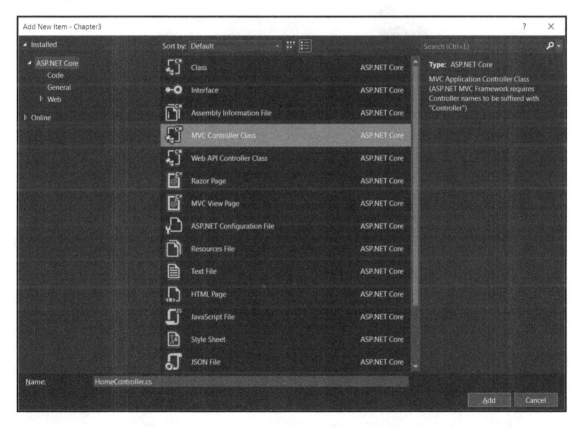

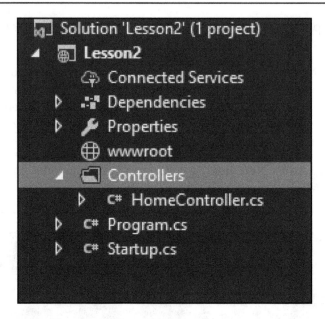

A class will be created with the following content:

```
public class HomeController : Controller
{
  // GET: /<controller>/
  public IActionResult Index()
  {
    return View();
  }
}
```

All controllers, both MVC and Web API controllers, inherit from the `Controller` base class. In earlier versions of ASP.NET MVC, MVC controllers would inherit from the `Controller` class and Web API controllers would inherit from the `APIController` class.

In the preceding `HomeController` class, we have a single action method by `Index` that returns the corresponding view. When you run the application as it is, you'll get a **500 Internal Server Error**. The reason for this is that no view has been created for the `Index` action of the `HomeController` and ASP.NET Core tries to search for that view. As the view is not available, it returns a **500 Internal Server Error** with the message **"InvalidOperationException: The view 'Index' was not found. The following locations were searched:"**. Whenever a status code starts with `5XX`, then we think that it is the servers, fault. Whenever a status code starts with `4XX`, then it is client related.

Instead of creating and returning that view, let us make a simple change to this action method. Let us return a string, **Hello World! I am learning MVC!**, and change the return type of IActionResult:

```
public string Index()
{
    return "Hello World! I am learning MVC!";
}
```

Run the application. You'll see the **Hello World! I am learning MVC!** in your browser, as shown in the following screenshot. Please make sure that you remove the app.Run statement in the Configure method, as mentioned earlier:

Voila! We have changed the ASP.NET Core application to render the custom content instead of the boring **Hello World!** What we have done may seem like a marginal improvement, but we have used controllers and action methods in our ASP.NET Core application, which has brought a lot of structure and flexibility to the web application development.

The following screenshot shows what happens in the background when we run the application:

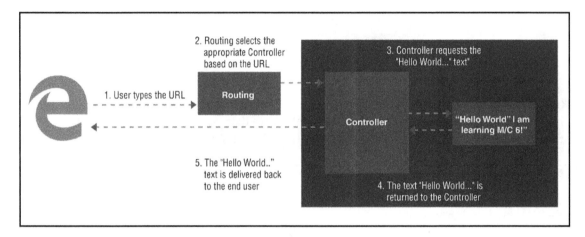

The following is the sequence of steps that occur when we run the application:

1. The application runs on the URL `http://localhost:50140`, where `50140` is the port number selected by IIS Express to run the application on my local system. This number may vary.

2. As we have not passed any parameter, default values for the `Controller` and action methods will be selected. In our case, `HomeController` will be chosen as the `Controller` and `Index` will be chosen as the action method in the `HomeController`. Since `ID` is the optional value and it is not passed, this `ID` parameter is ignored.

3. After the `Controller` and `action` methods are selected by the routing engine, control is passed to the `action` method of the selected controller. In our case, it will be the `Index` action method of the `HomeController`.

4. In the `Index` action method, we are returning a string, **Hello World! I am learning ASP.Net MVC!** This text is returned from the controller, which would then return back to the user.

IActionResult

If you noticed, the default return type in the `action` method of the controller was `IActionResult`, and then we changed the return type to the string in order to return the text **Hello World!**.

The `IActionResult` is the interface that we can use to return different types of `ActionResult`, ranging from a simple string to complex JSON data, so, we don't need to change the return type of the `action` method to return the string.

In the earlier example, the return type was changed to the string to make things simple. Now, let us make a simple change to return the string by keeping the return type (`IActionResult`) as it is:

```
// GET: /<controller>/
public IActionResult Index()
{
  return Content("Hello World! I am learning MVC!");
}
```

While returning the string, we are using the virtual method called `Content` from the `Controller` class (the base controller from where `HomeController` is inherited from) in the preceding `action` method. The purpose of this `Content()` method is to convert the string to the type `IActionResult`.

`IActionResult` is capable of returning different data types:

- `ContentResult`: Can return a text result.
- `EmptyResult`: Returns a null result.
- `FileResult`: Returns a binary output to write to the response.
- `HttpStatusCodeResult`: Provides a way to return.
- `JavaScriptResult`: Returns a script that can be executed from the client side.
- `JSonResult`: Returns a serialized JSON object.
- `RedirectResult`: Redirects to another action method.
- `RedirectToRouteResult`: Represents a result that performs a redirection by using a specified route values dictionary.

 These are actually methods in the `ControllerBase` class.

Activity: Implementing Your Own IActionResult

Scenario

You want to learn how to access the underlying stream of response of a string.

Aim

Write an activity result that would capitalize the given string.

Steps for completion

1. First, add the following class to your projects:

 Go to `https://goo.gl/GDi6JS` to access the code.

```
public class UpperStringActionResult : ActionResult
{
  readonly string str;
  public UpperStringActionResult(string str)
  {
    this.str = str;
  }
  public override void ExecuteResult(ActionContext context)
  {
    var upperStringBytes =
    Encoding.UTF8.GetBytes(str.ToUpper());
    context.HttpContext.Response.Body.Write(
    upperStringBytes, 0, upperStringBytes.Length);
  }
}
```

 What is encoding? Encoding is basically a process in which a sequence of characters is put into a specialized format. The characters could be numerical, alphabet, symbols, and so on. The purpose is to serve efficient transmission and storage. What is UTF-8? UTF-8 is the encoding for the web for efficiency reasons.

2. Then, revise your controller action, as follows:

 Go to `https://goo.gl/DTWzN4` to access the code.

```
public IActionResult IndexUpper()
{
    return new UpperStringActionResult("Hello World! I am learning
MVC!");
}
```

3. Then, run your application. You'll get the following output:

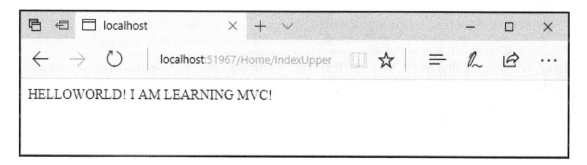

As you can see, all letters are in capitals.

Adding Views

So far, we were returning a simple string from the controller. Although that explains the concept of how the `Controller` and `action` methods works, it is not of much practical use.

Let's create a new `action` method named, `Index2`:

 Go to `https://goo.gl/UhaHyz` to access the code.

```
public IActionResult Index2()
{
    return View(); // View for this 'Index2' action method
}
```

Now, we have created the `action` method that returns a view, but we have still not added the view. By convention, ASP.NET MVC would try to search for our view in the `Views\{ControllerName}\{ActionMethod.cshtml}` folder. With respect to the preceding example, it will try to search for `Views\Home\Index2.cshtml`. Please note that the name of the `controller` folder is `Home`, not `HomeController`. The prefix is only needed as per convention. As this folder structure and file are not available, you'll get a **500 Internal Server Error** when you try to access this action method through the URL `http://localhost:50140/Home/Index2`.

So, let us create a folder structure. Right-click on the solution, navigate to **Add** | **New Folder** from the context menu, create a folder called Views, and then create a subfolder by the name Home within the Views folder:

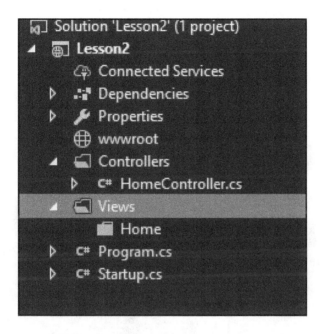

Right-click on the `Home` folder, and navigate to **Add | New Item** from the context menu. A dialog will appear, as shown in the below screenshot. Give the name of the file as `Index2.cshtml`, as our `action` method name is `Index2`. `cshtml` is the Razor view engine (this will be discussed in detail in *The View Engine* and the *Razor View Engine* section of the next chapter) extension used when you are using C#.

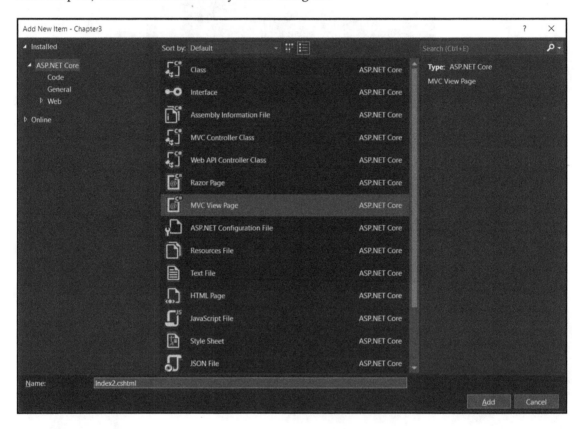

A file by the name `Index2.cshtml` will be created with the following content when you click on the **Add** button in the preceding screen:

`@*` is the comment syntax in the Razor view engine. You can write any C# code within the `@{}` block.

Let us add a simple HTML block after the generated code:

```
<html>
<body>
   Hello! This is <b>my first View</b>
</body>
</html>
```

Now, when you run the application, you will get the following output:

The following diagram explains the request flow and how we generate the response through the View:

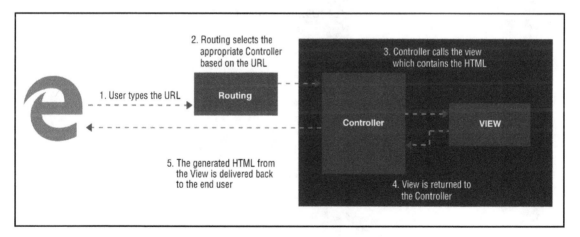

Adding Models

Models represent your business domain classes. Now, we are going to learn about how to use the Models in our controller. Create a `Models` folder and add a simple `Employee` class. This is a just a plain old C# class:

 Go to `https://goo.gl/uBtpw3` to access the code.

```
public class Employee
{
  public int EmployeeId { get; set; }
  public string Name { get; set; }
  public string Designation { get; set; }
}
```

Create a new `action` method, `Employee`, in our `HomeController`, and create an object of the `Employee` Model with some values, and pass the Model to the View. Our idea is to use the Model employee values in the View to present them to the user:

 Go to `https://goo.gl/r4Jc9x` to access the code.

```
public IActionResult Employee()
{
  //Sample Model - Usually this comes from database
  Employee emp1 = new Employee
  {
    EmployeeId = 1,
    Name = "Jon Skeet",
    Designation = " Software Architect"
  };
  return View(emp1);
}
```

Now, we need to add the respective View for this `action` method. Add a new Razor view file called `Employee.cshtml` in the `View\Home` folder.

Add the following code snippet. Whatever comes after the @ symbol is considered as Razor code. In the following code, we are trying to access the properties of the Model object that is passed to our view. In our case, Model represents the employee object that we have constructed in our action method. You can access the object from the view using the Model keyword:

Go to https://goo.gl/u4gCzN to access the code.

```
<html>
<body>
  Employee Name : @Model.Name <br />
  Employee Designation: @Model.Designation <br />
</body>
</html>
```

When you run the application and type the URL http://localhost:50140/Home/Employee, you'll see the following output:

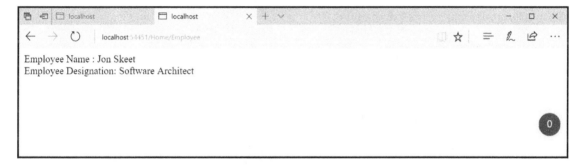

Optional: Take Up a Challenge

Alter your View code so that it displays EmployeeID.

Try to display a non-existing property such as @Model.Age. What happens when you do it?

Note that we get an error message if we try to access a non-existing property.

Passing Data from the Controller to the View

We have just discussed how to pass the data from the controller to the view using the `Model` object. While calling the view, we are passing the model data as a parameter. But there are times when you want to pass some temporary data to the view from the controller. This temporary data may not deserve a `model` class. In such scenarios, we can use either `ViewBag` or `ViewData`.

`ViewData` is the dictionary and `ViewBag` is the dynamic representation of the same value.

Let us add the company name and company location property using `ViewBag` and `ViewData`, as shown in the following code snippet:

 Go to `https://goo.gl/oYH7am` to access the code.

```
public IActionResult Employee()
{
   //Sample Model - Usually this comes from database
   Employee emp1 = new Employee
   {
     EmployeeId = 1,
     Name = "Jon Skeet",
     Designation = " Software Architect"
   };
   ViewBag.Company = "Google Inc";
   ViewData["CompanyLocation"] = "United States";
   return View(emp1);
}
```

Make the respective changes in the `Employee.cshtml` View file as well so that we can display the `Company` name and `CompanyLocation` values:

 Go to `https://goo.gl/KmqUhx` to access the code.

```
<html>
<body>
   Employee Name : @Model.Name <br />
   Employee Designation: @Model.Designation <br />
   Company : @ViewBag.Company <br />
   Company Location: @ViewData["CompanyLocation"] <br />
</body>
</html>
```

Run the application after making the preceding changes:

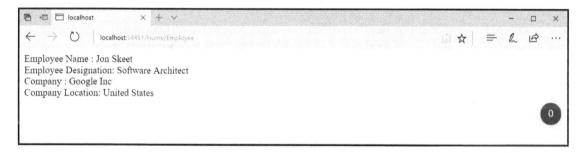

`ViewBag` and `ViewData` represent the same collection, even though the entries in the collection are accessed through different methods. `ViewBag` values are dynamic values and are executed at runtime, whereas the `ViewData` is accessed through the dictionary.

To test this, let us make a simple change to our `view` file:

```
<html>
<body>
   Employee Name : @Model.Name <br />
   Employee Designation: @Model.Designation <br />
   Company : @ViewData["Company"] <br />
   Company Location : @ViewBag.CompanyLocation <br />
</body>
</html>
```

Even though the `Company` value was stored using `ViewBag` in the `Controller`, we're accessing it using `ViewData`. The same is the case for the `CompanyLocation` value. We have stored the value using `ViewData` in the Controller, but we are accessing the value using `ViewBag`.

When you run the application after making the preceding changes, you'll see the same result as you have seen before.

Filters

Filters in ASP.NET MVC enable you to run code before or after a particular stage in the execution pipeline. They can be configured globally, per controller, or per action. You can consider filters as interceptors.

There are different kinds of filters, and each filter is executed at a different stage in the pipeline. For example, action filters are executed when the `action` method is executed.

Let us use a simple example to see how an action filter (a type of filter) works.

We've created a simple controller, `DateController`, where we're just displaying the time. In this `action` method, we're using a predefined action filter by the name of `ResponseCache`, that caches the response for the duration specified in seconds. In the following code snippet, we have mentioned the duration as `600` seconds. So, the response will be cached for 10 minutes:

 Go to `https://goo.gl/pEBqt6` to access the code.

```
public class DateController : Controller
{
    [ResponseCache(Duration = 600)]
    public IActionResult Index()
    {
        return Content(DateTime.Now.ToShortTimeString());
    }
}
```

When we run it for the first time, it displays the time as expected. But when you refresh the browser (which indirectly fires the request again), the time is not updated as the response is cached already by the application.

In the following screenshot, even though the time is 7:43, the application is still showing as 7:40:

Now, we'll look at some of the predefined types of filters available in ASP.NET Core.

Here are some of the different kinds of filters:

- **Authorization filters**: These are used for authorization and are mainly intended to determine whether the current user is authorized for the request being made.
- **Resource filters**: These are the filters that handle the request after authorization and are the last ones to handle the request before it leaves the filter pipeline. They are used to implement caching or by passing the filter pipeline.
- **Action filters**: These wrap calls to individual `action` method calls and can manipulate the arguments passed in the action as well as the action result returned from it.
- **Exception filters**: Exception filters are used to manage the unhandled exceptions in ASP.NET MVC.
- **Result filters**: Result filters wrap the individual action results and they only run when the `action` method is executed successfully.

With the help of caching we can immediately return results that are calculated previously, thus totally avoiding executing the request-response pipeline. The disadvantage is that we would be showing stale data.

Activity: Writing a Custom Filter

Scenario
You need to write a filter that will only allow the applied action on Sundays. How would you do that?

Aim
To write a custom filter.

Steps for completion

1. Open your editor and write this code:

Go to `https://goo.gl/9QKgbS` to access the code.

```
public class SundayFilter : Attribute, IActionFilter
{
  public void OnActionExecuting(ActionExecutingContext context)
  {
    if (DateTime.Now.DayOfWeek != DayOfWeek.Sunday)
    context.Result = new ContentResult()
    {
      Content = "Sorry only on sundays!"
    };
}
  public void OnActionExecuted(ActionExecutedContext context)
  {
  // do something after the action executes
  }
}
```

Setting results in the filter causes short circuiting, so our action does not run.

2. Now, we can apply this attribute onto our actions:

 Go to `https://goo.gl/x1ij7Z` to access the code.

```
[SundayFilter]
public IActionResult Employee()
{
...
...
}
```

You have successfully created a custom filter.

Summary

In this chapter, we have built our first ASP.NET Core application from scratch. We have learned how the controller fits into the overall ASP.NET MVC application and learned how to build our first controller with the `action` methods. We also learned how to use the model and view in our controller. We have also discussed different ways to pass the data from the controller to the view using `ViewBag` and `ViewData`. We have also learned about filters in ASP.NET MVC and how to make use of predefined filters in ASP.NET Core.

3
Views

Views are the actual output of an application which are delivered to the user. They are what users actually see on the screen when they access your application. All components, including menus, input elements, dialog boxes, and everything else the user sees come from your views. If you do not provide a good user experience when accessing your application, users will not care how great your application is. So, views play a critical role when building an ASP.NET MVC application. Separating views from a controller allows the HTML design process to be separate from the logic. It is also beneficial in terms of unit testing the controller.

By the end of this chapter, you will be able to:

- Explain the purpose of the view engine and the Razor view engine
- Program in the Razor view engine and use different programming constructs
- Work with the layout in ASP.NET Core and its features
- Generate HTML code
- Create and call partial views
- Create a view component
- Create custom Tag Helpers

The View Engine and the Razor View Engine

As discussed in Chapter 1, *Setting the Stage*, a browser can only understand HTML, CSS, and JavaScript. The purpose of the view engine is to generate the HTML code from your view and send it to the browser so that it can understand the content. Primarily, there are two different types of view engines—the Razor view engine and the Web Form view engine. Although these two view engines come out of the box with ASP.NET MVC, you can use any custom view engine.

The Razor View Engine

The Razor view engine is the default and recommended view engine in ASP.NET Core. Going forward, it may be the only view engine that comes out of the box when you install ASP.NET MVC.

You can mix C# code and HTML code in your Razor view and the Razor view engine is intelligent enough to distinguish between the two and generate the expected output. In some scenarios, you may have to give additional information to the Razor view to produce appropriate results. Razor code blocks start with the @ symbol but do not require a closing @.

Programming in the Razor View Engine

Programming in the Razor view engine is just like programming in C#. The difference is that, in the Razor view engine, your C# code will be mixed with HTML to produce the desired HTML output.

Variables in the Razor View

You can declare a variable inside the Razor block and use that variable using the @ symbol.

> In all the examples in this chapter, we will only present the code samples of the view.

Working with Razor View

Here's an example for us to explore Razor view. Follow these steps:

1. Create a new empty ASP.NET Core project.
2. Create a `Controllers` folder and a controller called `HomeController`.
3. Create a folder called `Views`, a subfolder called `Home`, and a view file called `Index.cshtml` by right-clicking on the context menu, navigating to **Add | New Item**, and then selecting **MVC View Page** from the list.

According to the pattern of configuration over convention, the controller name must match the appropriate view folder. Hence, we name the controller `HomeController` and the view folder `Home`.

4. Make sure your `Startup.cs` file looks as follows:

Go to `https://goo.gl/qzz2aT` to access the code.

```
public class Startup
{
    // This method gets called by the runtime. Use this method to add
services to the container.
    // For more information on how to configure your application,
visit
    https://go.microsoft.com/fwlink/?LinkID=398940
    public void ConfigureServices(IServiceCollection services)
    {
        services.AddMvc();
    }
    ...
    ...
}
```

5. The `HomeController.cs` file will have the following code:

Go to `https://goo.gl/vWxjRq` to access the code.
When copying code from the link provided, remember to append it with the closing curly brace for the `HomeController` class, as shown in the preceding code snippet.

```
public class HomeController : Controller
{
    // GET: /<controller>/
    public IActionResult Index()
    {
        return View();
    }
}
```

Next is the updated MVC view page, where we will declare a variable and use it. The first five lines and the last two lines are simple HTML elements.

We will concentrate on the lines that are bold. Then, we will create a Razor block using @ {
... } and declare a variable inside it. The Razor block ends with the closing curly bracket.
The snippet `Value:` is considered simple HTML text. As we would like to use the Razor
variable value, we will use `@i` to instruct the Razor view engine that `i` is not normal HTML
text; it is a Razor construct and is to be treated accordingly. The complete HTML code is as
follows:

 Go to `https://goo.gl/Jch17b` to access the code.

```
<html>
<head>
  <title> Views demo</title>
</head>
<body>
  @{
     int i = 5;
  }
  Value: @i
</body>
</html>
```

When you run the application, you'll see the following output:

When you access the Razor variable, you will need to use the @ symbol. Without this, the Razor view engine sees the i variable as text and not as an expression.

The following screenshot is the result you will get when you access the variable without the @ symbol:

Programming Constructs in the Razor View

You can use most of the programming constructs available in C# in the Razor view. Let's look at some of these in detail.

The for Loop

Writing code for the for loop is pretty straightforward. Let's write a piece of code for the for loop construct.

Here's the code for the for loop construct where we loop through the file five times and print the variable name:

```
@{
    for (int i = 0; i < 5; i++)
    {
        <li>@(i + 1)</li>
    }
}
```

The following are a few points to note:

- As the `for` loop is Razor code, we should begin the loop with an @ symbol to indicate that the code that follows is Razor code and not normal HTML.
- Whenever we use an HTML element or tag, the Razor view engine falls back to HTML mode. If you want to use a Razor expression within HTML tags, you need to include the @ symbol again to tell the Razor view engine that whatever follows is Razor code and not an HTML element. This is the reason we use the @ symbol again in the preceding expression, even within the parent root-level Razor code.

 Razor is a template engine. We use Razor expressions on the dynamically generated HTML parts.

The complete code for the view is as follows:

```
<html>
<head>
  <title> Views demo</title>
</head>
<body>
  <ul>
  @{
    for (int i = 0; i < 5; i++)
    {
      <li>@(i + 1)</li>
    }
  }
  </ul>
</body>
</html>
```

The while Loop

Let's write a piece of code for the `while` loop. We'll implement the same loop we used for the previous example. Please note that the emboldened expressions increment the variable `i`. We will not use the @ symbol, as it is not within the HTML element.

Here's the code for the `while` loop construct where we loop through the file five times and print the variable name:

```
@{
    int i = 0;
    while (i < 5)
    {
        <li>@(i + 1)</li>
        i++;
    }
}
```

The foreach Loop

The `foreach` loop in the Razor view is the same as the `foreach` loop in C#.

Here's the code for the `foreach` loop construct where we initialize a list of integers, iterate through the list, and print it as a list item:

```
<ul>
    @{
        List<int> integers = new List<int>
        {
            1,2,3,4,5
        };
        foreach (int i in integers)
        {
            <li>@i</li>
        }
    }
</ul>
```

The if Condition

Let's look at an example of the `if` condition; we will check whether the value of the variable is less than 10. If it is less than 10, we will print **i is less than 10**, otherwise, we will say **i is greater than 10**. You may wonder why we have to include the text tag and what its purpose is.

As we are inside the Razor view code block, the text **i is less than 10** will be considered a Razor expression, but it is not.

This `text` tag is to instruct the Razor view engine that whatever follows the `text` tag is to be considered as text and not a Razor expression.

Here's the code for the `if` condition to check whether the value of the variable is less than 10 or not:

```
@{
  int i = 5;
  if (i < 10)
  {
    <text>i is less than 10</text>
  }
  else
  {
    <text>i is greater than 10</text>
  }
}
```

Activity: Printing Prime Numbers from 1 to 100

Scenario

You're working on a project that calculates different mathematical formulae. You start with a basic one that prints prime numbers.

Aim

Write a view that prints the prime numbers from 1 to 100 to the browser.

Steps for completion

Use a function called `IsPrime` along with the `@function` declaration, as follows:

 Go to `https://goo.gl/pCLuFD` to access the code.

```
@functions
{
  public bool IsPrime(int n)
  {
    if (n <= 1) return false;
    if (n <= 3) return true;
    if (n % 2 == 0 || n % 3 == 0) return false;
    for (var i = 5; i * i <= n; i = i + 6)
      if (n % i == 0 || n % (i + 2) == 0)
      return false;
    return true;
  }
}
<ul>
...
...
</ul>
```

Layout

In all the previous examples we have discussed, we did the complete view coding in a single file. This results in a lack of flexibility and reduced reusability.

Consider the following web page structure, where the **Top Section** contains the company logo or banner and the **Side Section** contains links to various sections of the site. The **Content Section** changes for every page:

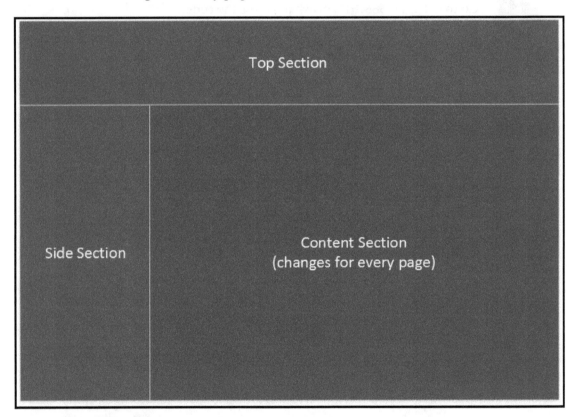

If we code the complete content in a single view, we may have to duplicate the **Top Section** and **Side Section** on every page. If we want to change anything in the **Side Section**, we will have to change all the files. This clearly shows that a single view file is not the best solution.

The layout comes to the rescue in this scenario, defining the site structure, which can be reused across all web pages. The layout does not need to have a top section or side section; it can contain a simple HTML structure, where you can have common content and the body content will be rendered from the individual view.

We can use HTML frames instead of the layout. However, when we use HTML frames, each frame becomes isolated, appearing as completely separate pages.

Building our First Layout

In order to use the layout, follow these steps:

1. **Get the name of the layout file**: This information should be made available in _ViewStart.cshtml. By convention, the names of all shared files will start with an underscore, and this file is located directly under the Views folder.

2. **Create the layout file**: By convention, the name of the file is _Layout.cshtml and it will be located in the Shared folder. All shared content, such as partial views, will also be available here. Partial views will be discussed later in this chapter.

3. **Create the content view file**: This view file is almost the same as the view files that we created earlier, with only one difference; only page-specific content will be available in this file, and this means that you'll not have any html, head, or title tags here. The folder structure looks as follows:

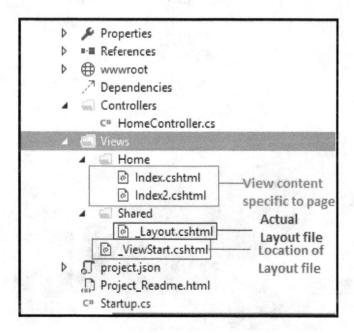

The `project.json` file is deprecated and will be missing in new projects. After the creation of `_ViewStart.cshtml`, `_Layout.cshtml`, and page-specific view files, the folder structure will look like the preceding screenshot.

Creating _ViewStart.cshtml

The `_ViewStart` file can be used to define common view code that you want to execute at the start of each view's rendering. Because this code executes at the start of each view, we no longer need to explicitly set the layout in any of our individual view files.

Right-click on the **Views** folder and select **Add New Item** from the context menu. Then, select **MVC View Start Page** from the **Add New Item** dialog box, as shown in the following screenshot:

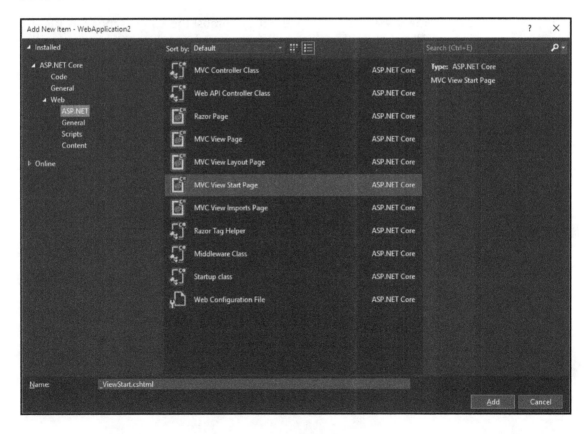

When you click on the **Add** button, it will create a file with the following content:

```
@{
    Layout = "_Layout";
}
```

Creating _Layout.cshtml

Create a folder called `Shared` within the `Views` folder. Then, right-click on the `Shared` folder and select **Add New Item** from the context menu, as shown in the following screenshot:

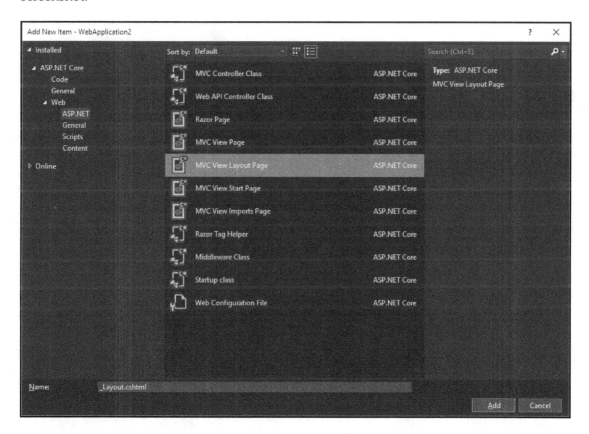

When you click on the **Add** button, it will create _Layout.cshtml with the following content:

```
<!DOCTYPE html>
<html>
<head>
  <meta name="viewport" content="width=device-width" />
  <title>@ViewBag.Title</title>
</head>
<body>
  <div>
  @RenderBody()
  </div>
</body>
</html>
```

The preceding layout file is simple HTML content with a couple of Razor expressions. @ViewBag.title is used to display the title information passed from the controller and @RenderBody is the Razor expression that calls the page-specific view and merges that content over there.

Adding a Page-Specific View

Let's add a page-specific view. Before adding the view, we will need to add an action method in our HomeController file, from which we will call our page-specific view. Follow these steps to add a page-specific view:

1. Let's add an action method named Index2, as follows:

 Go to https://goo.gl/xMK1zK to access the code.

```
public IActionResult Index2()
{
  ViewBag.Title = "This is Index2";
  return View();
}
```

ViewBag is used to pass information from the controller to the view. Here, we are passing the Title information from the action method to the view. Remember, ViewBag and ViewData are key value collections that you can fill from your controller and use from your view side. ViewBag is a dynamic object, whereas ViewData is a string key-value pair.

2. Now, right-click on the **Views** folder, navigate to **Add | New Item**, select **MVC View Page**, and save the file as Index2.cshtml. In the generated view, we've added simple Hello text. This text will be rendered in the body of the layout page. The complete code of the view file is as follows:

Go to https://goo.gl/vePWui to access the code.

```
@*
For more information on enabling MVC for empty projects,
visit https://go.microsoft.com/fwlink/?LinkID=397860
*@
@{
}
Hello. This text will be rendered in body of the layout
page
```

3. Everything is set now. Run the application and type the URL http://localhost:50132/Home/Index2 in the browser.

The port number after the localhost may vary when you run the application from your PC.

You will get this output:

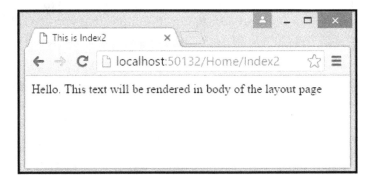

As expected, you'll see the text shown in the preceding screenshot. However, our point is not about the text, it's about the structure of the generated HTML content.

4. View the source by pressing *Ctrl + U* (on the Chrome browser in Windows). You'll see the following HTML content:

The top content (the `html`, `head`, `body`, and `div` opening tags) and bottom content (the `html`, `body`, and `div` closing tags) come from the layout file and the text comes from the view specific to the page.

Activity: Creating Another Layout and Changing the View to That Layout

Scenario

You've created a layout for your website. You're required now to create another layout and change the view to that layout by your company.

Aim

To create another layout and then dynamically change the view to that layout when we hit our action method.

Steps for completion

1. First, we write the following code to our action method:

Go to https://goo.gl/Jo2NQu to access the code.

```
public IActionResult Index()
{
    var view = View();
    view.ViewData["Layout"] =
    "~/Views/Shared/_Another.cshtml";
    return view;
}
```

2. Then, we modify our _ViewStart.cshtml file, as follows:

Go to https://goo.gl/WQqWvn to access the code.

```
@{
    Layout = (string)ViewData["Layout"] ?? "_Layout";
}
```

We have dynamically changed our layout!

Generating HTML

As discussed in `Chapter 1`, *Setting the Stage,* browsers can understand only HTML, CSS, and JavaScript, irrespective of the technology that you use to build the web application. This holds true when building the application in ASP.NET MVC as well.

Most applications get the user input, process the input, and then store the required information in the database to retrieve it later. In the context of web applications, HTML form elements are used to get user input.

The **HTML Helpers** and **Tag Helpers** are a couple of ways to generate HTML elements in ASP.NET Core.

HTML helpers are server-side methods that aid in the generation of HTML elements that can be understood by browsers. HTML helpers were the primary method of generating HTML elements up until ASP.NET MVC 5.

Tag Helpers, introduced in ASP.NET Core, also produce HTML elements. Tag Helpers, which we will discuss in a later section of this chapter, look just like HTML elements, where you add attributes to identify them as Tag Helpers. The advantage of using Tag Helpers over HTML helpers is that user interface designers/engineers do not need to worry about Razor code; they just code with HTML elements and additional attributes.

Before discussing HTML helpers and Tag Helpers, let's take a step back and talk about why we need them in the first place.

Generating HTML using a Simple Form

Consider a simple form, as shown in the following screenshot, where we would like to get the user's name and their age. If the user enters their age and it is equal to or greater than 18, we will display **You are eligible to vote!** If not, we will display **You are not eligible to vote now**:

The following is the HTML code to show the preceding simple form:

 Go to `https://goo.gl/f59Ep8` to access the code.

```html
<form>
  <table>
    <tr>
      <td>
        <label for="txtName">Name</label>
      </td>
...
...
      <td colspan="2">
        <input type="submit" />
      </td>
    </tr>
  </table>
</form>
```

This method of coding HTML elements directly is time-consuming and error-prone. For example, in the preceding form, the label and input HTML elements refer to the same element (`txtName` in the first group and `txtAge` in the second group). If we hand-code the HTML element, there is the possibility of a typo error in building the HTML element.

HTML Helpers

HTML Helpers are server-side methods that generate HTML for you.

Generating a form using HTML Helpers

We can generate the same form using HTML Helpers as follows (`HTML.BeginForm`, `@Html.Label`, and `@Html.TextBox` generate the HTML form, label, and textbox elements, respectively):

```csharp
@using (Html.BeginForm())
{
  <table>
    <tr>
      <td>@Html.Label("Name")</td>
      <td>@Html.TextBox("txtName")</td>
    </tr>
```

```
    <tr>
      <td>@Html.Label("Age")</td>
      <td>@Html.TextBox("txtAge")</td>
    </tr>
    <tr>
      <td colspan="2"><input type="submit" value="Submit">
      </td>
    </tr>
  </table>
}
```

 The `form` tag will automatically close when you use the block.

The following screenshot gives a glimpse of the task of HTML Helpers:

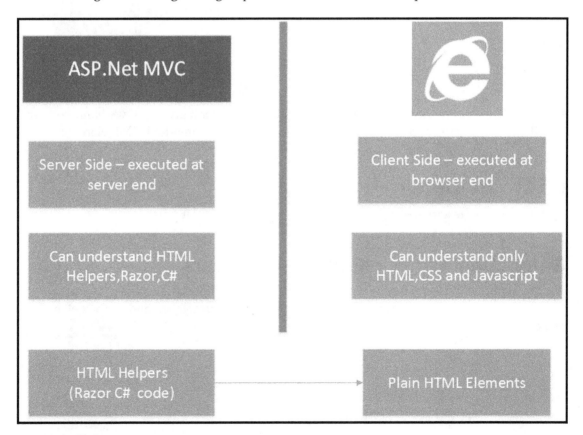

You might wonder why we need to use HTML Helpers when we can write the HTML code manually. Things will become more complex when we pass the model from the controller to the view. Using HTML Helpers, we can directly build form elements from model files so that they will pick the names from the models that you are using.

For example, let's create a folder called `Models` and a class called `Person`. This class will act as a model, as shown in the following screenshot:

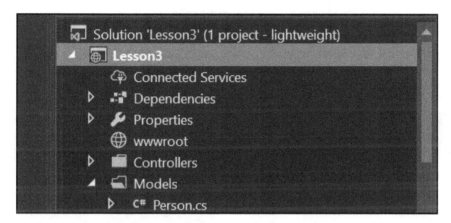

The `Person` class is just a **POCO (Plain Old C# Object)** class and will act as a model. The complete code for this class is as follows:

 Go to `https://goo.gl/UBmSdM` to access the code.

```
public class Person
{
    public int PersonId { get; set; }
    public string Name { get; set; }
    public int Age { get; set; }
}
```

Let's create a new `action` method called `ValidateAge`. In this method, we will create an empty `Person` class and pass the model to the view. We will also create a dynamic property called `Title` in `ViewBag` so that we can display this value in the view:

Go to `https://goo.gl/xCkyeY` to access the code.

```
[HttpGet]
public IActionResult ValidateAge()
{
  ViewBag.Title = "Validate Age for voting";
  Person person1 = new Person();
  return View(person1);
}
```

In the view, create the form using the following HTML Helpers:

 Go to `https://goo.gl/hnkvzS` to access the code.

```
@model Lesson3.Models.Person
@using (Html.BeginForm("ValidateAge", "Home", FormMethod.Post))
{
  <table>
    <tr>
      <td>@Html.LabelFor(Model => Model.Name) </td>
      <td>@Html.TextBoxFor(Model => Model.Name) </td>
    </tr>
    <tr>
      <td>@Html.LabelFor(Model => Model.Age)</td>
      <td>@Html.TextBoxFor(Model => Model.Age)</td>
    </tr>
    <tr>
      <td colspan="2"><input type="submit" value="Submit">
      </td>
    </tr>
  </table>
}
```

In the first line, we tell the view that we are passing the model of type `Person` class. This enables us to use a strongly typed model, that is, when we type `Model` and a dot, **IntelliSense** provides us with all the properties of the `Person` class.

Strongly typed model is beneficial, besides IntelliSense because if in the future you rename the properties of your model, you will detect these errors at compile time.

In the second line, we use the overloaded `BeginForm` HTML Helper, which accepts three parameters—the action method name, the controller name, and the `Form` method.

Simply put, when the user submits the form, the information should be passed to the mentioned action of the controller.

In the `LabelFor` and `TextBoxFor` HTML Helpers, we are just passing model properties (name and age); this automatically queries and gets the model properties and builds the respective HTML elements. This is one of the primary advantages of using HTML Helpers. Without using HTML Helpers, this process might become complex.

Now, let's write the respective `POST` action method in the same way. In the following `POST` action method, based on the age entered in the form, we set the dynamic property as `Message`:

 Go to `https://goo.gl/e4cB6j` to access the code.

```
[HttpPost]
public IActionResult ValidateAge(Person person1)
{
    if (person1.Age >= 18)
    {
        ViewBag.Message = "You are eligible to Vote!";
    }
    else
    {
        ViewBag.Message = "Sorry.You are not old enough to vote!";
    }
    return View();
}
```

We are using POST instead of GET because our goal is not to retrieve data, but to post and process data on the server side.

It should be noted that both the `GET` and `POST` action methods refer to the same view—`ValidateAge.cshtml`. Add the following content to the view just above the form element:

Go to `https://goo.gl/6Cx4fg` to access the code.

```
@if (ViewBag.Message != null)
{
  <b>@ViewBag.Message</b>
}
```

Once the user submits the form, the POST action method sets the dynamic `Message` property in `ViewBag`. However, the value of this property will be null when the view is rendered as part of the `GET` request. If the value is not null, insert the message at the top of the page.

When you run the application, you'll get the following output:

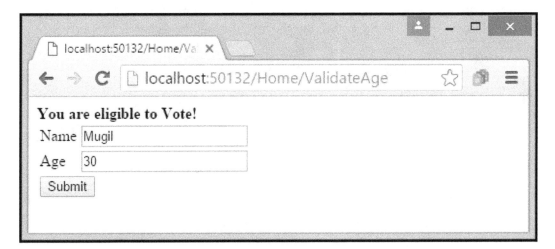

Activity: Making Use of a Checkbox

Scenario

Your fields for your web page is ready. Now, you're asked to make use of a checkbox for the age option instead of entering the age, as shown:

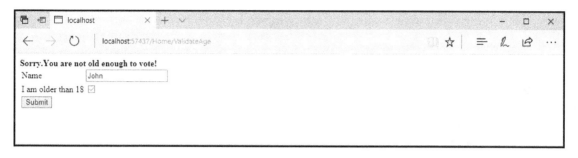

Aim

Make use of a checkbox for the age option instead of entering the age.

Steps for completion

1. Use the following code to change your view:

Go to `https://goo.gl/WtzFSg` to access the code.

```
@model Activity3C1.Models.Person
@if (ViewBag.Message != null)
{
   <b>@ViewBag.Message</b>
}
@{
}
@using (Html.BeginForm("ValidateAge", "Home",
FormMethod.Post))
{
   <table>
     <tr>
       <td>@Html.LabelFor(Model => Model.Name) </td>
       <td>@Html.TextBoxFor(Model => Model.Name) </td>
     </tr>
...
...
...
   </table>
}
```

2. Change your action using the following code:

Go to `https://goo.gl/Fqkrg3` to access the code.

```
[HttpPost]
public IActionResult ValidateAge(Person person1)
{
  if(Convert.ToBoolean(
  Request.Form["OlderThan18"][0]))
  {
    ViewData["OlderThan18"] = true;
    ViewBag.Message = "You are eligible to Vote!";
  }
  else
  {
    ViewBag.Message = "Sorry.You are not old enough to vote!";
  }
  return View();
}
```

The reason we use `Request.Form["OlderThan18"][0]` is that, by default, the checkbox
helper creates a hidden form, meaning that we get a false value if the checkbox is
unchecked. As HTML, by default, does not send a value for unchecked checkboxes, we also
fill our `ViewBag` so that we can retain our value.

Partial View

Partial views are views that can be reused across your application. Partial views can be
thought of as pluggable, reusable blocks that you can call from anywhere and have the
content of the partial view displayed. The difference between layouts and partial view is
that layouts surround our pages, whereas partial views are contained within our pages.

Consider the following structure of a web page—it's the same layout page that we used
earlier, but with a couple of changes. The **Latest News** block has been added to the **Side
Section** and the **Login** block has been added to the **Top Section**. These blocks are not
restricted to the **Top Section** or **Side Section** and can be used anywhere in your
application, including your **Content Section**, as shown in the following figure:

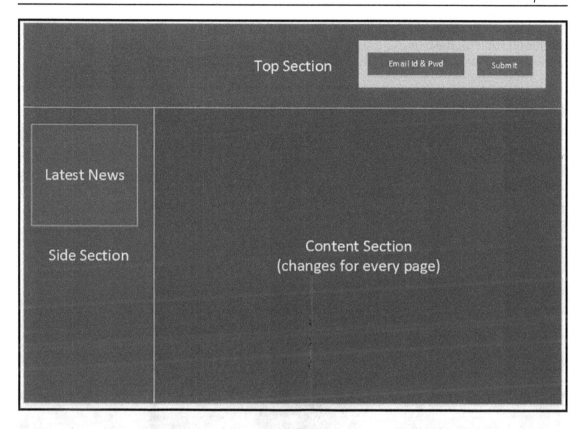

These partial views are not restricted to static content and can contain form elements. In the preceding screenshot, the **Latest News** partial view contains the text content and the login partial view contains form elements to get an e-mail ID and password.

The framework does not restrict the location of the partial view. However, by convention, if your partial view will be used only by your controller, you can create that partial view in the controller-specific Views folder. For example, if your partial view will only be used in the HomeController file, you can create that partial view in the Views folder under Home.

Let's take a look at how to create and use a partial view.

As discussed earlier, a partial view is just like a normal view. So, we will create a partial view in the same way we created a normal view.

Right-click on the **Shared** folder and navigate to **Add** | **New Item**. By convention, as with all shared content, the name of the partial view will also start with "_"(underscore), as shown in the following screenshot:

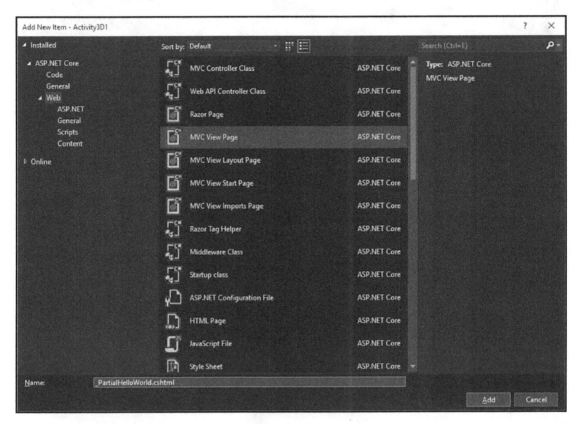

 We are creating this partial view based on the assumption that it can be used from anywhere in the application.

To add simple static content—text and a simple table—in the generated partial view, use the following code snippet:

```
<b>This content and below table is coming from partial view</b>
<table border="1">
  <tr>
    <th>Employee No</th>
    <th>Employee Name</th>
  </tr>
  <tr>
    <td>10012</td>
    <td>Jon Skeet</td>
  </tr>
  <tr>
    <td>10013</td>
    <td>Scott Guthrie</td>
  </tr>
</table>
```

Calling a Partial View

A partial view can be called using the `@Html.Partial` HTML helper.

In our case, we will be calling the partial view from the `Index2.cshtml` file. The parameter that you pass will be the name of the partial file. It will search for the partial view by that name and render that complete content as part of the `Index2.cshtml` file.

The content of the `Index2.html` file will now be as follows:

 Go to `https://goo.gl/1nRe4M` to access the code.

```
Hello. This text will be rendered in body of the layout page<br />
<br />
<br />
@Html.Partial("_PartialHelloWorld")
```

Now, run the application and access the URL `http://localhost:50132/Home/Index2`. You'll see the following output:

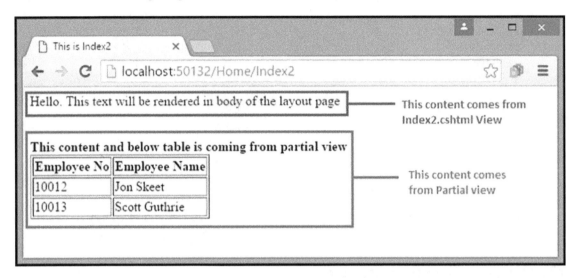

Also, look at the other overloads of `@Html.Partial` by right-clicking and selecting `Peek Definition`. This will allow you to pass a model or a copy of `ViewBag`. We say a copy because changes to the bag within the partial view do not propagate back to the parent.

Activity: Working with Static Data

Scenario

You're working on implementing the MVC pattern in your project. You want to generate static data from the action and pass it to the partial view as a model.

Aim

Generate static data from the action and pass it to the partial view as a model.

Steps for completion

1. We first create an `Employee` model object:

 Go to `https://goo.gl/j9N4BV` to access the code.

```
public class Employee
{
    public int Id { get; set; }
    public string Name { get; set; }
}
```

2. Then we return the data from the action:

Go to `https://goo.gl/hAuXfB` to access the code.

```
public IActionResult Index2()
{
    var employees = new List<Employee>
    {
        new Employee { Id = 10012 , Name = "John Skeet"},
        new Employee { Id = 10013 , Name = "Scott Guthrie"},
    };
    return View(employees);
}
```

3. We then pass the data to the partial view from `Index2.cshtml`, as follows:

Go to `https://goo.gl/ZYirD8` to access the code.

```
@model List<Activity3D1.Models.Employee>
Hello. This text will be rendered in body of the layout
page<br /> <br /> <br />
@Html.Partial("_PartialHelloWorld", @Model)
```

4. And finally, render the HTML from the partial view:

Go to `https://goo.gl/cj2aeR` to access the code.

```
@model List<Activity3D1.Models.Employee>
<b>This content and below table is coming from partial
view</b>
<table border="1">
    <tr>
```

```
      <th>Employee No</th>
      <th>Employee Name</th>
   </tr>
   @{
      foreach (var employee in Model)
      {
        <tr>
          <td>@employee.Id</td>
          <td>@employee.Name</td>
        </tr>
      }
   }
</table>
```

View Components

View components are a new feature introduced in ASP.NET Core. They are similar to partial views; however, they are more powerful in nature.

When you use partial views, you have a dependency on the controller. However, when you use the `ViewComponent` attribute, you do not have to depend on the controller. So, we are able to establish a separation of concerns and have better testability. Even though the existing partial view HTML Helper is still supported, it is preferable to use the view component whenever you want to show a reusable piece of information when you are using .NET Core.

Creating a View Component

You can create a view component using any of the following methods:

- Create a class by deriving one from the `ViewComponent` attribute
- Enhance a class with the [`ViewComponent`] attribute or derive it from the class that has the [`ViewComponent`] attribute
- Use the convention by creating a class that ends with a suffix `ViewComponent` attribute

Whichever option you choose, the view component should be a public, non-nested, and non-abstract class.

As with controllers, you can use dependency injection (via a constructor) in the `ViewComponent` attribute too. As the `ViewComponent` attribute is separate from the controller life cycle, you may not be able to use the action filters in `ViewComponents`.

There is a method called `Invoke` (or `InvokeAsync`, the asynchronous equivalent of `Invoke`), that will return the `IComponentViewResult interface`. This method is similar to the `action` method of the controller that will return the view.

Creating a ViewComponent Attribute

Follow these steps to create a `ViewComponent` attribute:

1. Create a new folder called `ViewComponents` in your project and a new class called `SimpleViewComponent`, as shown in the following screenshot:

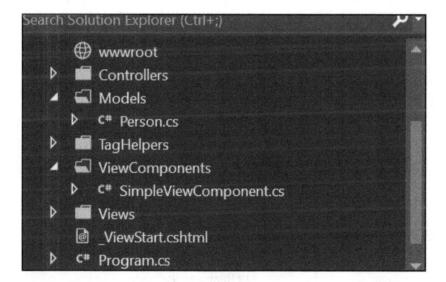

The `SimpleViewComponent` file that we created will look like the following:

```
using Microsoft.AspNetCore.Mvc;
using System;
using System.Collections.Generic;
using System.Linq;
using System.Threading.Tasks;
namespace Lesson3.ViewComponents
{
    public class SimpleViewComponent : ViewComponent
```

```
{
    public IViewComponentResult Invoke()
    {
...
...
    }
  }
}
```

Go to `https://goo.gl/4KAXW8` to access the code.

2. We have just a couple of methods: one to populate the data and the `Invoke` method, where we will render the view. Once you have created the `ViewComponent` attribute, you will need to include the `ViewComponent` namespace in the `_ViewImports.cshtml` file under `Views` so that the `ViewComponents` attributes are available for all the views. The highlighted code snippet in the following is added to the view:

Go to `https://goo.gl/pK9tau` to access the code.

```
@using Lesson3
@using Lesson3.ViewComponents
@addTagHelper "*, Microsoft.AspNet.Mvc.TagHelpers"
```

3. We have created the `ViewComponents` and made them available to all of the views. A simple action method in the `HomeController` file just returns the view:

Go to `https://goo.gl/EYmx7M` to access the code.

```
public ActionResult Sample()
{
    return View();
}
```

4. In the associated view, we can invoke the component, as shown in the following code snippet:

Go to `https://goo.gl/cbQnR3` to access the code.

```
<p>
  This is a sample web page <br />
  <div>
    @await Component.InvokeAsync("Simple")
  </div>
</p>
```

When you invoke the component, it will search in the following two folders:

- The `<view name>` folder under `Views\Shared\Components\<view_component_name>`
- The `<view_name>` folder under `Views\Shared\Components\<view_component_name>`

5. The default view name of the view component is `Default`, which makes your filename for the view `Default.cshtml`. So, we will need to create the `Default.cshtml` file in the `Views\Shared\Simple\Default.cshtml` folder, as shown in the following screenshot:

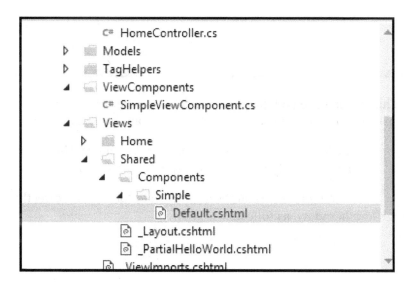

Go to `https://goo.gl/ELUVkG` to access the code.

In the view (the `Default.cshtml` file) of the `ViewComponent` file, we are just iterating the items in the model and displaying them as an unordered list item, as shown in the following code:

```
@model IEnumerable<string>
<h3> Sample list</h3>
<ul>
  @foreach (var item in Model)
  {
    <li>@item</li>
  }
</ul>
```

When you run the application and access the URL (`http://localhost:50132/Home/Sample`), you should see the following output:

The first line, **This is a sample web page**, comes from the parent view file (`sample.cshtml`), whereas the subsequent list comes from the `ViewComponent` attribute.

The `ViewComponent` attributes are usually referred to in the views. However, if you want to call the `ViewComponent` directly from your controller, you can do so.

We call the `Sample` action method to call the Simple `ViewComponent` directly instead of calling it through another view, as follows:

Go to `https://goo.gl/X6e2Xm` to access the code.

```
public ActionResult Sample()
{
   return View("Simple");
}
```

Thus, these view components have far more flexibility and features, such as dependency injection, when compared to old HTML partial views. This ensures view components are separately testable.

Activity: Passing a String as Additional Data

Aim

To pass additional data to our view component at the time of invocation by using one of its overloads. So, let's pass the Four string as additional data so that the output will be as shown in the following screenshot:

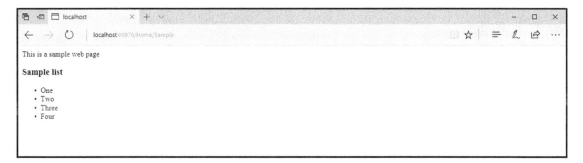

Steps for completion

1. We modify our view as follows:

Go to `https://goo.gl/rxkDYt` to access the code.

```
<p>
   This is a sample web page <br />
   <div>
      @await Component.InvokeAsync("Simple", new { additionalData =
"Four" } )
   </div>
</p>
```

2. Then, modify our `ViewComponent` as follows:

Go to `https://goo.gl/XhCkmZ` to access the code.

```
using Microsoft.AspNetCore.Mvc;
using System;
using System.Collections.Generic;
using System.Linq;
using System.Threading.Tasks;
namespace Lesson3.ViewComponents
{
   public class SimpleViewComponent : ViewComponent
   {
...
...
   }
}
```

Tag Helpers

Tag Helpers are a new feature in ASP.NET Core; they help generate HTML elements. In HTML helpers, we will write C#/Razor code to generate HTML. The disadvantage associated with this approach is that many frontend engineers will not know C#/Razor code; they work with plain HTML, CSS, and JavaScript. Tag Helpers look just like HTML code, but have all the features of server-side rendering. You can even build custom Tag Helpers as per your needs. The advantage of Razor over Tag helpers is that while Tag Helpers are more frontend-developer friendly, sometimes we might need the power of Razor, as it is a powerful programming model.

Let's take a look at how to use a Tag Helper. The Tag Helpers package is already included in the `Microsoft.AspNet.Core.All NuGet` package.

Remember, we have already added Tag Helpers support to the `ViewImports` file in the preceding section.

Had we included the `_ViewImports.cshtml` file under the `Home` folder, Tag Helpers would be available only for the views under the Home folder. So, we should use the root of the view folder.

Let's add a simple action method called `Index3` in the `HomeController` file, and in the associated view, we will use Tag Helpers, as shown in the following code:

 Go to `https://goo.gl/zwYvmh` to access the code.

```
public IActionResult Index3()
{
    ViewBag.Title = "This is Index3";
    Person person = new Person();
    return View(person);
}
```

Add the corresponding view (the `Index3.cshtml` file) for the `Index3` action method with the following code:

 Go to `https://goo.gl/s545Nw` to access the code.

```
@model Lesson3.Models.Person
<form asp-controller="Home" asp-action="Index3">
  <table>
    <tr>
      <td><label asp-for ="Name">Name</label></td>
      <td><input asp-for="Name" /></td>
    </tr>
    <tr>
      <td><label asp-for ="Age">Age</label></td>
      <td><input asp-for ="Age" /></td>
    </tr>
    <tr>
      <td colspan="2"><input type="submit" value="Submit"/></td>
    </tr>
  </table>
</form>
```

The following are a few things that you need to note in the preceding code for the use of Tag Helpers:

- All the form elements look just like standard HTML elements, with just a few changes to the attributes. This enables frontend developers to work independently without learning HTML/Razor code, thus more easily achieving a separation of concerns.
- The first line of the preceding view indicates the type of model data passed to the view from the controller.
- The `form` element has a couple of attributes, named `asp-controller` and `asp-action`, which represent controller names and action method names respectively.
- The `label` and `input` Tag Helpers are just like HTML elements, with just an additional `asp-for` attribute. The values for these attributes represent the model properties. You can take advantage of IntelliSense when entering the values for these attributes.

Custom Tag Helpers

ASP.NET Core provides many built-in Tag Helpers to help you create the necessary HTML elements for many scenarios. However, they do not cover all scenarios. Sometimes, you may want to make some changes to a generated HTML element, or you may want to create an HTML element with new properties, or a new HTML element altogether. You are not restricted to using the existing Tag Helpers in the ASP. NET Core application. You can create your own Tag Helper if the existing Tag Helpers do not suit your needs. Let's create a simple Tag Helper to create an email link:

```
<a href="mailto:mugil@dotnetodyssey.com">
```

There are a couple of ways to create Tag Helpers: by implementing the `ITagHelper` interface or inheriting the `TagHelper` class. The `TagHelper` class has a `Process` method that you can override to write custom Tag Helpers. The `TagHelper` class also has the `TagHelperOutputparameter`, which you can use to write and generate the desired output HTML. So, it is preferable to create Tag Helpers by inheriting from the `TagHelper` class.

Our objective is to write a custom email Tag Helper so that when someone uses that Tag Helper, which is `<email mailTo="mugil@greatestretailstore.com"></email>`, it is converted to the following line of code:

```
<a href="mailto:mugil@greatestretailstore.com">Drop us a mail</a>
```

Creating a Custom Tag Helper

The following are the steps that need to be performed to create a custom Tag Helper in the ASP.NET Core application:

1. Create a folder called `TagHelpers` and add a new item named `EmailTagHelper.cs`. By convention, all Tag Helper classes should end with `TagHelper`, even though we can override this convention:

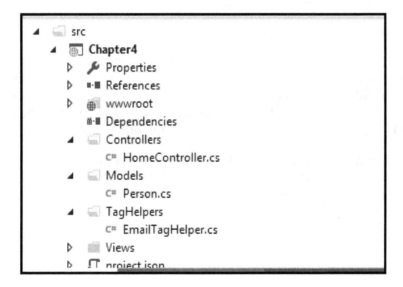

2. Once you have created the file, you will need to override the `Process` method to generate the desired HTML output:

Go to `https://goo.gl/xNJoqB` to access the code.

```
using Microsoft.AspNetCore.Razor.TagHelpers;
using System;
using System.Collections.Generic;
using System.Linq;
using System.Threading.Tasks;
namespace Lesson3.TagHelpers
{
  public class EmailTagHelper : TagHelper
  {
```

```
    public override void Process(TagHelperContext context,
...
...
    }
}
```

The parameters used in the preceding code are explained as follows:

- The context parameter provides all the information that you supplied in the Tag Helper. For example, in the `<emailmailTo="mugil@greatestretailstore.com"></email>` Tag Helper, you can get the `mailTo` attribute and its associated value from the `context` parameter. In the first line of the preceding `Process` method, we will get the `mailTo` attribute value and use that value to create an attribute in the generated HTML (anchor tag).
- The `output` parameter is of type `TagHelperOutput`, which is used to generate the desired HTML output.
- The `output.Content.SetContent` parameter will set the text that is to be displayed for the anchor tag.

3. We have created the email Tag Helper. Now, we have to make it available to our views so that we can make use of that Tag Helper in them. Edit `Views\_ViewImports.cshtml` to include the namespace of the `TagHelpers` and add the associated TagHelpers. In the following `_ViewImports.cshtml` file, we have added the content highlighted in bold:

```
@using Lesson3
@using Lesson3.ViewComponents
@addTagHelper "*, Microsoft.AspNet.Mvc.TagHelpers"
@addTagHelper "*, Lesson3"
```

The * symbol in the following line tells the view engine to include all the `TagHelpers` in the Lesson3 namespace:

```
@addTagHelper "*, Lesson3"
```

You can only include specific `TagHelpers`. For example, the following line will include only the `EmailTagHelper` so that it is available to our views:

```
@addTagHelper " Lesson3.TagHelpers.EmailTagHelper, Lesson3"
```

4. Let's create a simple action method in our Home controller. In the view of the associated action method, we will use the email Tag Helper:

```
public IActionResult AboutUs()
{

  return View();
}
```

The following is the view of the preceding `AboutUs` action method:

```
<h3>About Us</h3>
We are one of the biggest electronics retail store serving
millions of
people across the nation. blah.blah. blah <br />
If you want to hear great offers from us
<email mailTo="mugil@greatestretailstore.com"></email>
```

5. When you run the application and access the `http://localhost:50132/Home/AboutUs` URL, you will see the following output:

Here, we created an anchor tag with the `mailto` attribute and the email value as the `href` attribute value.

We open the Developer Tools window (Press *F12* to do this and select the **DOM Explorer** tab) to see the generated HTML.

You can find more samples at `https://github.com/dpaquette/TagHelperSamples`.

Activity: Replacing Email Tag Helpers

Scenario

You're maintaining an application for your company. The company wants to get rid of all the email Tag Helpers from the code. How will you do it?

Aim

Replace the `EmailTagHelper` so that we can use it like the following:

```
<email> mugil@greatestretailstore.com </email>
```

Steps for completion

Use the following code:

Go to `https://goo.gl/VCdwpB` to access the code.
We can still use HTML attributes on Tag Helpers, as in:
`<email style="color:red"`
`mailTo="mugil@greatestretailstore.com"></email>`
This will render the link in red.

```
public class EmailTagHelper : TagHelper
{
   public override async Task ProcessAsync(TagHelperContext context,
TagHelperOutput output)
...
...
}
```

Summary

In this chapter, you learned what a view engine is and how to build a view using the Razor view engine. We also discussed the different programming constructs that you can make use of in Razor to produce the desired HTML output. Then, you learned about layout and how to provide a consistent site structure across all of the pages in your ASP.NET MVC application. Later in the chapter, we discussed how to promote reusability using partial views, with an example. Finally, you learned how to use Tag Helpers to produce clean HTML.

4
Models

Data is at the heart of every application. A user enters data into the application, edits the entered data, and searches the data. We can even say that an application that we build is just an interface for the operations that we perform on the application data. So, it is absolutely necessary for any framework to provide a mechanism to make data operations easier and more manageable. Models in ASP.NET MVC are used to represent the business domain data.

By the end of this chapter, you will be able to:

- Explain models and their purpose
- Create a simple model and use it in the controller and views of the ASP.NET MVC application
- Create a model specific to a ViewModel
- Use data flow in an ASP.NET MVC application in the context of models and ViewModels
- Explain the purpose of Entity Framework along with its features and benefits
- Add, update, and delete data using Entity Framework
- Use Entity Framework in ASP.NET MVC applications

Introduction to Models

Models are simple **POCO (Plain Old C# Objects)** classes representing your business domain data. They basically model real-world entities. We can consider them as code reflections of real-world concepts and entities. For an e-commerce business, model classes would be `Product`, `Order`, and `Inventory`. If you are building an application for a university, model classes would be `Student`, `Teacher`, and `Subject`. Models represent the business domain data in your application and they are not aware of the underlying database that is being used in your application. In fact, you don't even need a database to work with models.

Creating an ASP.NET Core Application

Here are the steps to create an ASP.NET Core application:

1. Make sure to create an ASP.NET Core application with an empty template.
2. Create a `Controllers` folder and create a `HomeController` with a single `Index` action method.
3. Create the following folder/files for the ViewModel:
    *   `Views`: This folder is inside your project.
    *   `Views\_ViewStart.cshtml`: This identifies the name of the `Layout` file.
    *   `Views\Shared`: This folder holds all the shared view components for your application.
    *   `Shared\_Layout.cshtml`: This file identifies how your web application structure should look.
    *   `Views\Home`: This folder contains all of the Views of your `HomeController`.
    *   `Views\Home\Index.cshtml`: This is the view corresponding to the Index action method of `HomeController`.
4. And make sure your `Startup.cs` looks like the following:

 Go to `https://goo.gl/edbYJx` to access the code.

```
public class Startup
{
// This method gets called by the runtime. Use this method to add
services to the container.
// For more information on how to configure your application, visit
https://go.microsoft.com/fwlink/?LinkID=398940
public void ConfigureServices( IServiceCollection services)
...
...
}
```

Now, we have created an ASP.NET Core application with Controllers and Views.

Let us create a Models folder in our application; this folder will contain all of your model files. In a real-world application, this folder and the respective model files would reside in separate projects. For the sake of simplicity, we are keeping the Models folder and its files in the same project.

Let us create a simple Product model class, in the Models folder:

```
public class Product
{
    public int ProductId { get; set; }
    public string Name { get; set; }
    public decimal Price { get; set; }
}
```

This Product model class is no different from any other C# class and contains a few properties about the product.

Update the Index action method in HomeController to use the Product model, as shown in the following code snippet. We are building the model data and passing the model data to the view so that it can be shown to the users. However, it is *NOT* recommended to build the model data in the controller's action methods as it violates the separation of concerns. For the sake of simplicity only, we are building the model data in an action method:

 Go to https://goo.gl/Pobwwi to access the code.

```
public IActionResult Index()
{
    /* Build the products model. It is NOT RECOMMENDED to build models in
Controller action methods like              this.
    * In real world application, these models and the respective Data Access
Layer(DAL) would be in separate       projects.
    * We are creating it here to make things simpler to explain */
    List<Product> Products = new List<Product>
    {
...
...
    };
    return View(Products);
}
```

Update the corresponding `Index` view method to use the model data loop through each product and show it as an unordered list item. The `@model` in the first line represents the model metadata, the type of data being passed to the view. The model in the `foreach` loop represents the actual data itself, a list of products in our case:

 When copying from GitHub remember to remove the comments before the return statement and the curly brace.

```
@model List<Lesson4.Models.Product>
<ul>
  @foreach (var Product in Model)
  {
    <li>@Product.Name</li>
  }
</ul>
```

When you run the application, you'll get the following output:

We have successfully created a model and have used it in our controller and view.

Let us create a comparatively complex model class, `Order` (`Order.cs` in the `Models` folder), which contains a list of products and their total amount:

 Go to `https://goo.gl/p97rGp` to access the code.

```
public class Order
{
    public int OrderId { get; set; }
    public List<Product> Products { get; set; }
    public decimal Total { get; set; }
}
```

We choose decimal instead of double for the `Total` field because double is stored as binary in memory for efficiency. However, this makes some decimal numbers not representable, thus the computer does some rounding to approximate. On the other hand, decimal is stored exactly as we humans calculate. So decimals are good for monetary values. Double is good for scientific calculations.

Here's what your folder structure will look like:

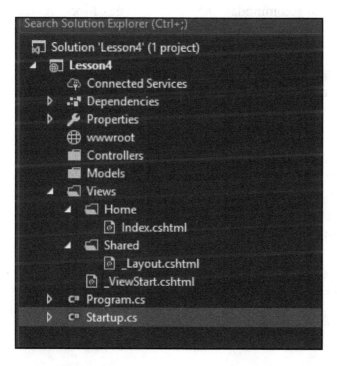

Now we have to update the `Index` action method to use the `Order` model. Once we build the list of products, we are assigning the products list to the `Order` property and calculating the total cost of the order. These calculations would usually be done as part of the business layer. Again, for the sake of simplicity, we are building the data model and calculations here in the action; this should never be the case in a real–world application.

The code highlighted in bold is the changes that we have made in the action method:

```
// GET: /<controller>/
public IActionResult Index()
{
...
...
    };
    Order order = new Order();
    order.Products = Products;
    order.Total = Products.Sum(product =>
    product.Price);
    return View(order);
}
```

The view is updated to accommodate the model changes. Model metadata (@model) is changed to indicate that the information of Order is passed to the view instead of the list of products.

Then, we are showing the list of products in table format. Please note that all of the model data (the Order object and its properties, in this case) can be accessed through the model. For example, the Products class can be accessed through Model.Products and the value of the Total can be obtained through Model.Total:

 Go to https://goo.gl/efhye6 to access the code.

```
@model Lesson4.Models.Order
<table border="1">
  <tr>
    <th>Product Name</th>
    <th>Price</th>
  </tr>
  @foreach (var Product in Model.Products)
...
...
</table>
```

When you run the application, you'll see the following output:

Models Specific to a View Component

There are scenarios where you might want to update only a few properties in a large model or you might want to create a new model based on a few models. In such scenarios, it is better to create a new model specific to the view.

For example, let us assume that we are building a screen where you update the price of the product. This simple screen may contain only three properties: product ID, product name, and the price of the product. But the product's model may contain more than 30 properties to hold all details of the product, such as manufacturer, color, and size. Instead of sending the complete model with all the properties, we can create a new model specific to this view with only a few properties—ID, name, and price.

ViewModels

ViewModels are entities where, when you update the model, your view will get updated automatically and vice versa. In many online articles and even in some books, the authors refer to **ViewModels** when they actually mean **Models specific to the View**.

In ViewModels, binding is two-way: when you update either the model or the view, the other one will get updated automatically.

Let us consider a simple example. You have a form with various fields on the left-hand side and print preview on the right-hand side. In this case, whatever you type in real time in the form will be reflected immediately on the right-hand side. In such cases, you can use pure ViewModels when you type; your ViewModel will be updated and that ViewModel will be consumed in the right-hand side print preview. These pure ViewModels are being used in advanced JavaScript frameworks such as KnockoutJS and AngularJS.

In models specific to the view, we are binding in only one way, from the model to the view. Here, we are sending a model specific to the view instead of the generic model (which represents a business domain class).

However, in this course, we will be referring to models specific to a view as ViewModels for brevity. Unless otherwise specified, you should read all ViewModels as models specific to a view. So, I am making the same mistake made by other authors (which I don't intend to do).

Using ViewModels is entirely optional.

There are few drawbacks of using ViewModels. First, you have to create a new class for your ViewModel. Second, you need to write code that translates from ViewModel to view and vice versa. There are frameworks to automate this process, such as AutoMapper.

ViewModels is good practice wherever it makes sense since it reduces the coupling.

Data Flow with Respect to a Model

The following block diagram shows the data flow in an ASP.NET MVC application:

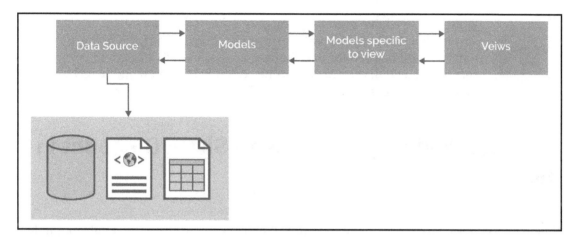

The two important aspects of data flow are as flows:

- **Data Source**: This represents your application data. The application data could reside anywhere—from full-fledged RDBMSes such as SQL Servers to simple Excel spreadsheets, or anything in between.
- **Models**: As previously mentioned, these represent the business domain data for your application and are independent of the data source being used. The same model could be used with different data sources.

We can use the **Model as-is in our views** to get data or to present it. In some views, you might not need all the properties of the model. So, instead of sending the entire model to the view, we create models specific to the view and use them in our view. This makes things simpler.

The following is the high-level sequence of events that happens when you store or retrieve a record in ASP.NET Core using the model:

1. Users enter the data in a form (created using views) in the application. The fields in the form do not need to represent the complete model as we need only a few properties in the model.
2. The entered data is passed to the controller where Model binding happens. Model binding is the process where the data entered in the view gets mapped to the model or ViewModel.

3. If the data is received in the ViewModel, then we will be converting the ViewModel to the model.

4. Finally, the model data is stored in the data source.

 Until now, we have been handling only in-memory data in our application. In almost all real-world applications, some form of the database will be used for data storage, access, and retrieval. In the next section, we will discuss Entity Framework (ORM framework), which makes data access simpler from a .NET application.

Activity: Revising the Code to Show Discount in the Total

Scenario

You want to revise the code so that it discounts the total sum by 10% if the total amount is larger than 1,000 and show this discount in the total.

Aim

Revise the code to show discount in the total.

Steps for completion

1. Change the Order class, as follows:

 Go to https://goo.gl/Q58VD2 to access the code.

```
public class Order
{
    public int OrderId { get; set; }
    public List<Product> Products { get; set; }
    public decimal Total { get; set; }
    public decimal Discount => Total > 1000M ? Total * 0.1M : Total;
}
```

2. Change the view, as follows:

 Go to `https://goo.gl/ScepWa` to access the code.

```
@model Lesson4.Models.Order
<table border="1">
  <tr>
    <th>Product Name</th>
    <th>Price</th>
  </tr>
  @foreach (var Product in Model.Products)
  {
  <tr>
    <td>@Product.Name</td>
    <td>@Product.Price</td>
  </tr>
  }
...
...
</table>
```

Model Binding

Model binding is the process of mapping the model data coming from the view to the ViewModel parameter of the action method in the controller.

Model binding eliminates the need to read the form data manually and assign it to the existing object. This would have been very tedious and error-prone. Model binding can also be enhanced and customized. It is a powerful mechanism to parse the incoming request automatically.

Let us consider a simple form with a couple of form fields: Name and EmailID. On submission of the form, these values would be mapped to the ViewModel object of the action method of the controller. Model binding takes care of this mapping. The model binder looks for a match in the form fields, query strings, and request parameters.

In the preceding example, any class with these properties would be picked up by ModelBinder without any issues.

As the following Person class contains the Name and EmailID properties, the model binder would not complain about using this model for mapping the entered values in the form:

```
public class Person
{
  public string Name { get; set; }
  public string EmailID { get; set; }
}
```

The following code snippet shows how to use the `Person` class in the action method:

```
public ActionResult Add(Person p)
{
  return View();
}
```

Entity Framework

If we are using a relational database, there is an impedance mismatch with the data and our domain classes, since the data is relational whereas our domain is composed of objects. The aim of using ORM is to eliminate (or hide) this mismatch so that we can totally ignore the persistence problems and instead focus on our code rather than trying to generate pesky SQL statements. Having said that, there are many valid cases to drop back to SQL statements, such as performance tuning cases or complex reports.

Entity Framework (EF) is the **Object Relational Mapping (ORM)** framework that enables developers to work on domain-specific objects directly for data access instead of working on database queries. This reduces a lot of the code complexity in the data access layer of the application.

Before discussing Entity Framework and its features, let us pause for a moment and think about the steps that we follow when we try to save some information to the database while using ADO.NET:

1. Construct the business domain object.
2. Create a connection to your database.
3. Open the connection.
4. Create a command object along with the command type.
5. Add the properties of your business domain object to the parameters of the command object.
6. Execute the command that saves the data into the database.

We have to follow these six steps for common operations such as saving a piece of data into the database.

If you are using an ORM framework such as Entity Framework, you just need three steps:

1. Construct the business domain object.
2. Create the `DbContext` class for your business domain object. The instance of the `DbContext` class represents the session with the database.
3. Save it to the database using the instance of the `DBContext` class.

You might wonder how that is possible.

As a matter of fact, in the background, Entity Framework creates a connection to the database and executes the query to save the business domain object to the database. To make it simple, Entity Framework writes all the data access code for you so that you can concentrate on achieving the business functionality of the application rather than writing the database layer code.

Entity Framework is Independent of ASP.NET MVC

As discussed earlier, Entity Framework is an ORM framework for accessing data and is independent of ASP.NET MVC. Entity Framework could be used in **Windows Communication Foundation (WCF)** services, Web API services, and even in console applications. You could use Entity Framework in any type of application and make use of it to access data using objects. The concepts and the functionalities of Entity Framework remain the same, irrespective of the type of application that you use it with.

Now, we are going to use Entity Framework with the console application. This allows us to concentrate on the task at hand and demonstrate the functionalities of Entity Framework instead of working on the boilerplate code of the ASP.NET Core application. In a later part of this chapter, we will integrate Entity Framework with the ASP.NET Core application.

The latest version of Entity Framework for the SQL server is EntityFrameworkCore. It brings significant changes when compared to its previous version (Entity Framework 6). However, EntityFrameworkCore is the recommended version when building ASP.NET Core applications, so we will be using that version in this book.

 We need a database to explain many of the features of Entity Framework. Before continuing, please use the following link to install SQL Server 2016 Express or (LocalDB)j or newer on your PC: `https://www.microsoft.com/en-us/sql-server/sql-server-editions-express`

Creating Console Applications with Entity Framework

Creating a console application with Entity Framework is what we'll look into next. Follow these steps to create a simple console application:

1. Navigate to **File** | **New Project** and select **Console App (.NET Core)**.

2. Name the project `ConsoleEF` and click on **OK**:

Installing Entity Framework Core NuGet Package

There are two ways to install any NuGet package in your application:

- Using the NuGet Package Manager

- Using the Package Manager Console

We'll look at the first option of using the NuGet Package Manager.

Using the NuGet Package Manager

People who prefer graphical interfaces can use this option:

1. Right-click on the console project and select **Manage NuGet Packages** from the context menu:

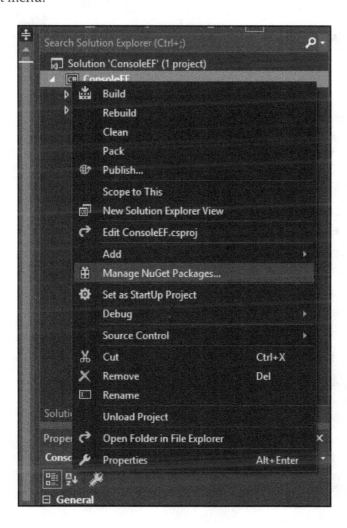

2. Search for `Microsoft.EntityFrameworkCore.SqlServer` in the NuGet package. Click on **Install** once you select **Microsoft.EntityFrameworkCore.SqlServer**:

3. Once you click on **Install**, the NuGet Package Manager will ask you to review the changes. Click on **OK**:

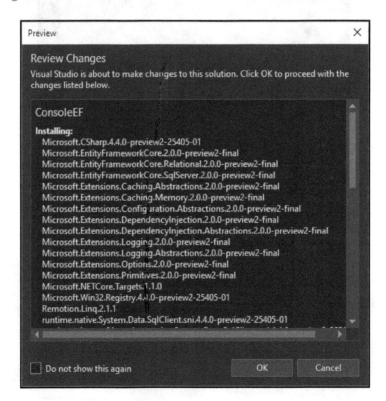

4. Click on **I Accept** in the **License Acceptance** window:

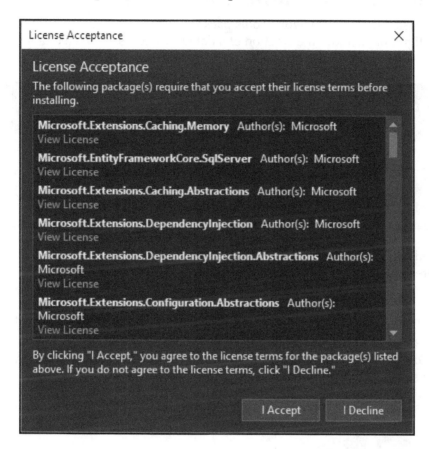

5. Once you click on **I Accept**, it will install Entity Framework with all its dependencies. In the Output window, you will get a **Finished** message once the installation is complete:

```
Time Elapsed: 00:00:03.0619983
========== Finished ==========
Restoring NuGet packages...
Time Elapsed: 00:00:00.3355224
========== Finished ==========
```

Installing Entity Framework Commands

We need to install Entity Framework Tools package in order to perform migration activities. Migration includes the creation of a database and its associated tables. Any changes in the schema will also be taken care of by migration:

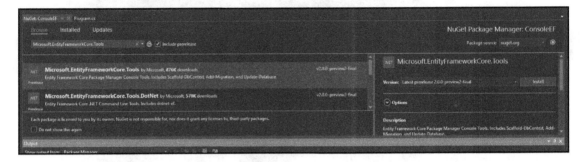

As discussed earlier, we need to follow three steps in order to interact with the database when we are using Entity Framework:

1. Create the model classes.
2. Create the `DbContext` class for your business domain object. The instance of the `DbContext` class represents the session with the database.
3. Construct the business domain object and save it to the database using the instance of the `DBContext` class.

Let us discuss each of the preceding steps in detail and try to save an object to the database.

Creating Model Classes

The `Model` classes are simple POCO objects that can be used with Entity Framework.

Let's create a POCO class for our business domain object, the `Employee` class in our case. Name the new file name `Employee.cs` in our console application. This `Employee` class contains a few properties of an employee and has no special properties or fields to make it work with Entity Framework.

Let's take a look at the following code snippet:

```
public class Employee
{
    public int EmployeeId { get; set; }
    public string Name { get; set; }
```

```
    public decimal Salary { get; set; }
    public string Designation { get; set; }
}
```

By convention, if the property name is `Id` or `ClassName+Id`, it will be considered as a primary key by the Entity Framework while creating the database table.

Properties with string data types will be created as fields of the `nvarchar(max)` type. However, we can override this behavior by using annotations, which will be discussed later.

Creating the DbContext Class

The instance of the `DbContext` class represents the session to the database and this `DbContext` class does most of the heavy lifting of your data access for your application. Create a new class named EmployeeDbContext with the following content:

 Go to `https://goo.gl/hbju3w` to access the code.

```
using Microsoft.EntityFrameworkCore;
namespace ConsoleEF
{
  public class EmployeeDbContext : DbContext
  {
    public DbSet<Employee> Employees { get; set; }
    protected override void OnConfiguring(DbContextOptionsBuilder
optionsBuilder)
    {
      optionsBuilder.UseSqlServer(@"Data Source=
      (localdb)\MSSQLLocalDB;Initial Catalog=
      EFConsole;Integrated Security=True;Connect
      Timeout=30;
        Encrypt=False;TrustServerCertificate=True;
        ApplicationIntent=ReadWrite;
        MultiSubnetFailover=False");
    }
  }
}
```

There are a few things to be noted in the preceding code snippet:

- Include the `Microsoft.EntityFrameworkCore` namespace as the `DbContext` class available in this namespace. Our connection string is currently hardcoded but we can easily make it configurable.

- In order to use the `DbContext` API, a class has to be created that inherits from the `DbContext` class so that we can access methods of the `DbContext` API. We have created the `EmployeeDbContext` class, which was inherited from DbContext class.

- `DbSet` is a class that allows operations of Entity Framework to be performed for a given Entity type. We need to create the `DbSet` object for each of the Entity types that we use in our application. In this example, we are using only one `DbSet` object as we are working with the `Employee` class.

Creating a Migration

Migration is the process of recording all the changes of your database. Writing migrations ensures that our database schema also evolves together with our application. It also solves versioning problems. If we have 10 customers and each is running a different version of our application, we don't have to track which schema is installed to which customer. Thanks to the automated process of migrations and migrations being part of the code itself, all we have to do is to run the migrations and it is guaranteed that the database schema will be in the correct state.

Follow these steps to create a migration:

1. `Add-Migration` is Entity Framework command for adding a migration, as shown here:

```
Package source: All              ⚙ Default project: ConsoleEF              ≣
Each package is licensed to you by its owner. NuGet is not responsible for, nor does it grant any licenses to, third-party packages. Some packages may include dependencies which
Follow the package source (feed) URL to determine any dependencies.

Package Manager Console Host Version 4.3.0.4273

Type 'get-help NuGet' to see all available NuGet commands.

PM> Add-Migration InitialMigration
To undo this action, use Remove-Migration.
PM> |
```

2. Once you add the migration, you can revoke the changes by executing the `Remove-Migration` Entity Framework command. This is what the `Migrations` directory looks like:

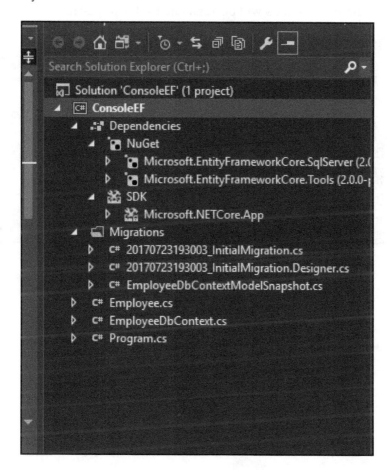

3. Update the database by issuing Entity Framework command `Update-Database`, which updates the database tables as per the information available in the migration. As we have installed the `EntityFramework.Commands` package earlier, these commands will be available for the application:

```
Package source:  All                    ⚙  Default project:  ConsoleEF

Each package is licensed to you by its owner. NuGet is not responsible for, nor does it grant any licenses to, third-pa
any dependencies.

Package Manager Console Host Version 4.3.0.4273

Type 'get-help NuGet' to see all available NuGet commands.

PM> Add-Migration InitialMigration
To undo this action, use Remove-Migration.
PM> Update-Database
Applying migration '20170723193003_InitialMigration'.
Done.
PM> |

100 %  ▾
Package Manager Console   C# Interactive   Error List   Output
```

4. Once you update the database, you can see the changes in the database by checking the SQL Server Object Explorer from the View menu:

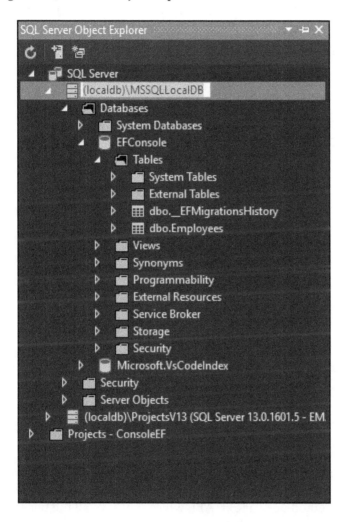

5. Perform the database operation to save the business domain object in the database. You can create the database manually or, if the database is not available, it will create one for you. The `Main` method is updated with the following code:

```
using System;
namespace ConsoleEF
{
  class Program
  {
    static void Main(string[] args)
    {
      AddEmployee();
    }
    static void AddEmployee()
    {
      using (var db = new EmployeeDbContext())
      {
        Employee employee = new Employee
        {
          Designation = "Software Engineer",
          Name = "Scott",
          Salary = 5600
        };
        db.Employees.Add(employee);
        int recordsInserted = db.SaveChanges();
        Console.WriteLine("Number of records inserted:" +
recordsInserted);
        Console.ReadLine();
      }
    }
  }
}
```

First, we are constructing the business domain object. Then, we are adding the constructed Employee object to the employee's `DbSet` of the `DbContext` class. Finally, we are calling the `SaveChanges` method `DbContext` API, which will save all the pending changes to the database.

You might be wondering how it can save it to the database when we have not even provided it with the connection string.

Let us discuss what happens behind the scenes when we run the program:

- When you make changes to any of the DbSet collection, Entity Framework checks whether the database exists. If it does not exist, it creates a new one using the <Namespace of DbContextName> pattern. In our case, a database called EF6.EmployeeDbContext would be created.
- Then, it creates database tables for the entities declared in DbSet. By convention, Entity Framework uses the pluralized form of Entity for the table names. As we have declared DbSet for the Employee entity, Entity Framework creates a pluralized form of Employee and creates the table named Employees.

The creation of the database and tables happens when the following code is executed:

```
db.Employees.Add(employee);
```

When the SaveChanges method is executed, the data in the Employee object will get saved to the database and return the number of records affected. In the preceding case, it returns 1.

When you run the application again, the first two steps mentioned previously will be skipped as the database and table will have already been created.

When you query the database, you can see the newly inserted record:

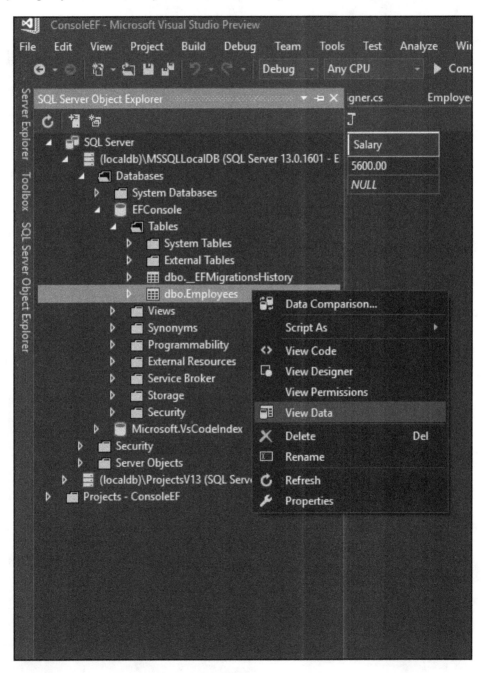

Here's the screenshot of the queried data:

	EmployeeId	Designation	Name	Salary
▷	1	Software Engin...	Scott	5600.00
◇	*NULL*	*NULL*	*NULL*	*NULL*

How the SaveChanges Method Works

When we are making changes, Entity Framework tracks the state of each of the objects and executes the appropriate query when the SaveChanges method is called. This relinquishes the developer from tracking what changed when changes for objects could be happening at different places of the code. It would have been very difficult for developers to track these changes by themselves.

The SaveChanges approach buys you transparent persistence, that is, your application would set data on a business object, and somewhere deep down below, in a lower layer, it would be saved, but automatically. The SaveChanges method is just flushing those tracked changes to the database, keeping memory and DB in sync.

For example, when we add an Employee object to the employees' collection (DbSet), this object is being tracked as Entity in the Addedstate. When SaveChanges is called, Entity Framework creates an insert query for it and executes it. The same is the case with updating and deleting the object. Entity Framework sets the Entity state of the respective objects to Modified and Deleted. When SaveChanges is called, it creates and executes the Update and Delete queries:

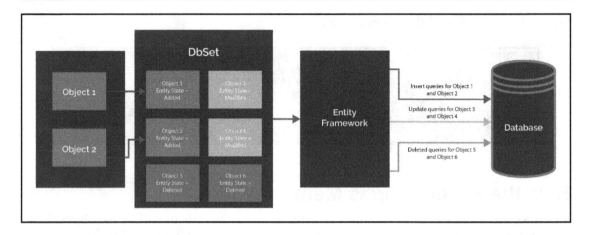

The preceding diagram explains how the SaveChanges method works at a high level for different types of change. We have a couple of POCO objects (**Object 1** and **Object 2**), which have been added to the employees DbSet object. Let us assume **Object 3** and **Object 4** have been modified and **Object 5** and **Object 6** are in the **Deleted** state. When you call the SaveChanges method, it creates three sets of queries. The first set of queries is for the addition of objects, resulting in the insert queries getting executed against the database. In the second set of queries, Update queries are created and executed for the objects whose state is modified. Finally, Delete queries are executed for all the **Deleted** state objects.

Updating the Record

Let us try to update the salary of an inserted employee record using Entity Framework:

 Go to https://goo.gl/4k5J6a to access the code.

```
static void UpdateSalary()
{
  using (var db = new EmployeeDbContext())
  {
    Employee employee = db.Employees.Where(emp
    => emp.EmployeeId == 1).FirstOrDefault();
    if (employee != null)
    {
      employee.Salary = 6500;
      int recordsUpdated = db.SaveChanges();
      Console.WriteLine("Records updated:" +recordsUpdated);
```

```
        Console.ReadLine();
    }
  }
}
```

In the preceding method, we find the employee with `EmployeeId = 1`. Then, we update the salary of the employee to `6500` and save the `employee` object to the database. Please note that, in the preceding method, we interact with the database a couple of times—once to find the correct employee record (read operation) and again to update the record (update operation):

```
static void Main(string[] args)
{
    UpdateSalary();
}
```

Also make sure you add `using System.Linq;` to the top of the file.

The `Main` method is updated to call the `UpdateSalary` method. When you query the database, you should see the record with the updated information:

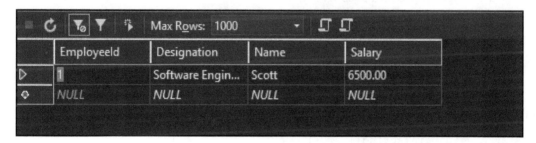

Make sure you click on the **Refresh** button.

Deleting the Record

Deleting the record is a bit tricky as it involves setting the state directly. In the following method, first we get the object and set the state of the object to Deleted. Using db.Delete method instead of setting a state would imply the record is deleted immediately from the database. However, this is not the case. The actual deletion will be pending until we call SaveChanges. Once we call the SaveChanges method, it will generate the delete query for the object and execute it, which in turn will eventually delete the record in the database:

 Go to https://goo.gl/QgqKCM access the code.

```
static void DeleteEmployee()
{
  using (var db = new EmployeeDbContext())
  {
    Employee employeeToBeDeleted =
    db.Employees.Where(emp => emp.EmployeeId ==1).FirstOrDefault();
    if (employeeToBeDeleted != null)
...
...
  }
}
```

Make changes in the Main method and ensure it looks like this:

```
static void Main(string[] args)
{
  DeleteEmployee();
}
```

Activity: Controlling the Transaction Manually

Aim

Control the transaction manually and commit it yourself.

Steps for completion

Here's the code:

 Go to `https://goo.gl/Wk9RUH` to access the code.

```
static void DeleteEmployee()
{
  using (var db = new EmployeeDbContext())
  using(var transaction =  db.Database.BeginTransaction())
...
...
}
```

Using Entity Framework in ASP.NET MVC Applications

There is not much difference between using Entity Framework in a console application and the ASP.NET MVC application. Now, we are going to build a simple application with a single screen, as shown in the following screenshot.

In this screen, we will have a form where the user will enter the information about the employee; once the user submits the form, the information will be saved to the database as shown in the following screenshot:

We can create a simple model for the employee. We need to build a ViewModel for this view, as we need to get the employee information from the user and we also need to show a list of employees on the same screen.

The following are the step-by-step instructions to create the application for the previously mentioned objective:

1. Create an ASP.NET Core project in Visual Studio by selecting an empty ASP.NET Core Web application.

2. All the Entity Framework packages we need come baked in, so there is no need to install anything.

3. Add an `appsettings.json` file by using Visual Studio, as shown here:

4. And change `appsettings.json` so that it resembles this:

```
{
  "ConnectionStrings":
  {
    "DefaultConnection": "Server=(localdb)
    \\MSSQLLocalDB;Database=Validation;
    Trusted_Connection=True;
    MultipleActiveResultSets=true"
  }
}
```

5. Configure MVC in the `Startup` class (`Startup.cs`):
   - In the constructor, we are building the configuration by reading the `appsettings.json` file.
   - Add the MVC service and the Entity Framework service to the services in the `ConfigureServices` method.
   - Configure the MVC routing in the `Configure` method:

 Go to `https://goo.gl/VezQkv` to access the code.

```
using System;
using System.Collections.Generic;
using System.Linq;
using System.Threading.Tasks;
using Microsoft.AspNetCore.Builder;
using Microsoft.AspNetCore.Hosting;
using Microsoft.AspNetCore.Http;
using Microsoft.Extensions.DependencyInjection;
using Microsoft.Extensions.Configuration;
using Microsoft.EntityFrameworkCore;
using MVCEF.Models;
namespace MVCEF
{
  public class Startup
  {
  ...
  ...
  }
}
```

6. Create the `Models` and `DbContext` classes.

7. Create the `Models` folder and add the `Employee` model class and `EmployeeDbContext` class.

8. Create the `Employee` model class (`Employee.cs` in the `Models` folder):

```
public class Employee
{
    public int EmployeeId { get; set; }
    public string Name { get; set; }
    public decimal Salary { get; set; }
    public string Designation { get; set; }
}
```

9. Create `EmployeeDbContext` (`EmployeeDbContext.cs` in the `Models` folder):

 Go to `https://goo.gl/G9Sm11` to access the code.

```
using Microsoft.EntityFrameworkCore;
using MVCEF.Models;
using System;
using System.Collections.Generic;
using System.Linq;
using System.Threading.Tasks;
namespace MVCEF.Models
{
    public class EmployeeDbContext : DbContext
    {
        public EmployeeDbContext(DbContextOptions<EmployeeDbContext>
options) :
        base(options)
        {
        }
        public DbSet<Employee> Employees { get; set; }
    }
}
```

10. Create ViewModels.

As we are going to show a list of employees and the form to add employees in the same screen, we are going to build a model specific to this view. This model will contain information about the list of employees and the employee to be added.

11. Create the `ViewModels` folder and add `EmployeeAddViewModel`.

Go to `https://goo.gl/Z7rSRa` to access the code.

```
using MVCEF.Models;
using System;
using System.Collections.Generic;
using System.Linq;
using System.Threading.Tasks;
namespace MVCEF.ViewModels
{
  public class EmployeeAddViewModel
  {
    public List<Employee> EmployeesList { get; set; }
    public Employee NewEmployee { get; set; }
  }
}
```

This `ViewModel` has a couple of properties: `EmployeesList` and `NewEmployee`. `EmployeesList` will contain the list of employees. This list will be fetched from the database. `NewEmployee` will hold the employee information entered by the user.

12. Create `Controllers` to handle the incoming requests:
   - Create a `Controllers` folder and add the `EmployeeController` class with a couple of action methods, one for `GET` and another for `POST`. The Index action method corresponding to the `GET` action method will be called when you access the URL (`http://localhost/Employee/Index`) or when you run the application. The `POST Index` action method will be called when you submit the form as the following:

Go to `https://goo.gl/Yivh8J` to access the code.

```
public IActionResult Index()
{
  EmployeeAddViewModel
  employeeAddViewModel = new EmployeeAddViewModel();
  var db = this.employeeDbContext;
  employeeAddViewModel.EmployeesList = db.Employees.ToList();
  employeeAddViewModel.NewEmployee = new Employee();
  return View(employeeAddViewModel);
}
```

- In the preceding GET Index action method, we are creating the ViewModel object and passing it to the view.
- The following code uses the POST Index action method:

 Go to https://goo.gl/gsoJnE to access the code.

```
[HttpPost]
public IActionResult Index(EmployeeAddViewModel
employeeAddViewModel)
{
  var db = this.employeeDbContext;
  db.Employees.Add(employeeAddViewModel.NewEmployee);
  db.SaveChanges();
  //Redirect to get Index GET method
  return RedirectToAction("Index");
}
```

- We get the NewEmployee property in the ViewModel, which contains the user's information. Save it to the database. Once we save the employee information to the database and we redirect the control to the GET Index action method, the GET Index action method will again show the form to enter the employee information and the list of employees in table format.
- Finally, we need to change the constructor so that our db context is injected:

```
readonly EmployeeDbContext
employeeDbContext;
public EmployeeController(EmployeeDbContext employeeDbContext)
{
  this.employeeDbContext = employeeDbContext;
}
```

Constructor parameter `EmployeeDbContext` comes from `services.AddEntityFrameworkSqlServer()`. Once this line is executed, we are basically instructing the runtime to inject this service wherever it is necessary within our controllers. This way, we don't have to keep track of it. When the request ends, the context returns to its own pool, waiting to be used.

- Our final code looks as follows:

Go to `https://goo.gl/eQHBT6` to access the code.

```
using System;
using System.Collections.Generic;
using System.Linq;
using System.Threading.Tasks;
using Microsoft.AspNetCore.Mvc;
using MVCEF.ViewModels;
using MVCEF.Models;
namespace MVCEF.Controllers
{
...
...
}
```

13. Add the `Views` folder.

14. Create `Views\_ViewStart.cshtml` with the following content:

```
@{
   Layout = "_Layout";
}
```

15. Create `Views\Shared\_Layout.cshtml` with the following content:

```
<html>
<head>
  <meta name="viewport" content="width=device-width" />
  <title>@ViewBag.Title</title>
</head>
<body>
  <div>
    @RenderBody()
  </div>
</body>
</html>
```

16. Create `Views\Employee\Index.cshtml` with the following content:

 Go to `https://goo.gl/Nf8kep` to access the code.

```
@model MVCEF.ViewModels.EmployeeAddViewModel
@*
//For more information on enabling MVC for empty projects, visit
http:
//go.microsoft.com/fwlink/?LinkID=397860
*@
@{
}
<div>
  @using (Html.BeginForm("Index", "Employee", FormMethod.Post))
  ...
  ...
</div>
```

In the preceding `Index` view, we create a form where we get the employee information from the user in the topmost `div` element. In the next `div` element, we show the list of employees in a tabular format.

Once we create all the folders and the files, the project structure should look like the following:

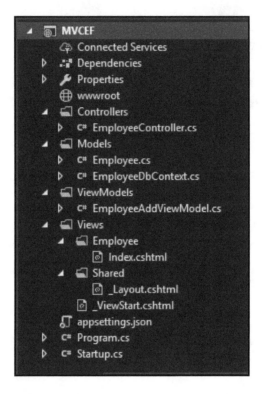

Revise the Index(EmployeeAddViewModel employeeAddViewModel) method

We'll look at revising the `Index(EmployeeAddViewModel employeeAddViewModel)` method so that it will first check whether an employee with the same name exists. If it exists, it will update that record instead.

Here's the code:

```
[HttpPost]
public IActionResult Index(EmployeeAddViewModel employeeAddViewModel)
{
  var db = this.employeeDbContext;
  var newRecord = employeeAddViewModel.NewEmployee;
  var existingEmployee =
  db.Employees.FirstOrDefault(k => k.Name == newRecord.Name);
  if (existingEmployee != null)
  {
    existingEmployee.Designation = newRecord.Designation;
```

```
        existingEmployee.Salary = newRecord.Salary;
    }
    else
    {
        db.Employees.Add(existingEmployee);
    }
    db.SaveChanges();
    //Redirect to get Index GET method return RedirectToAction("Index");
}
```

 The version might be different in your case.

Database Migration

We have created the business entity—the `Employee` class. Now, we can proceed with the migration. Migration is a two-step process: in the first step, we create the migration files. We have seen how to create migrations from the Package Manager Console. There is also one other way to create migrations from command-line tools. To do it, first we need to edit the `MVCEF.csproj` project file and add tools to the end of the file. So your project file's ending should look like this:

```
...
    <ItemGroup>
        <DotNetCliToolReference
Include="Microsoft.VisualStudio.Web.CodeGeneration.Tools"
        Version="2.0.0-preview2-final" />
        <DotNetCliToolReference
Include="Microsoft.EntityFrameworkCore.Tools.DotNet"
        Version="2.0.0-preview2-final" />
    </ItemGroup>
</Project>
```

Next, we will execute the command-line tools. This can be done by executing the following command from the Command Prompt from the context of the project:

dotnet ef migrations add InitialMigration

 `InitialMigration` is just a name. You can give it any name you like.

Finally, this command will create the migration files in your project, as shown in the following screenshot:

You will also see a model snapshot is created. This allows EF to get a new diff from your existing model so that as your model evolves, it can generate migrations for you.

The snapshot file has to be kept in sync with the migrations that create it, so you can't remove a migration just by deleting the file named _.cs. If you delete that file, the remaining migrations will be out of sync with the database snapshot file. To delete the last migration that you added, use the `dotnet ef migrations remove` command.

Then execute the following command to create the database:

```
D:\...\Lesson4\MVCEF\MVCEF>dotnet ef migrations add InitialMigration
info: Microsoft.AspNetCore.DataProtection.KeyManagement.XmlKeyManager[0]
      User profile is available. Using 'C:\Users\Onur.Gumus\AppData\Local\ASP.NET\DataProtection-Keys' as key repository and W
indows DPAPI to encrypt keys at rest.
Done. To undo this action, use 'ef migrations remove'
```

This command will read the migration files created in the previous step and create the database along with the associated tables:

```
D:\...\Lesson4\MVCEF\MVCEF>dotnet ef database update
info: Microsoft.AspNetCore.DataProtection.KeyManagement.XmlKeyManager[0]
      User profile is available. Using 'C:\Users\Onur.Gumus\AppData\Local\ASP.NET\DataProtection-Keys' as key repository and W
indows DPAPI to encrypt keys at rest.
info: Microsoft.EntityFrameworkCore.Database.Command[200101]
      Executed DbCommand (192ms) [Parameters=[], CommandType='Text', CommandTimeout='60']
      CREATE DATABASE [Validation];
info: Microsoft.EntityFrameworkCore.Database.Command[200101]
      Executed DbCommand (55ms) [Parameters=[], CommandType='Text', CommandTimeout='60']
      IF SERVERPROPERTY('EngineEdition') <> 5 EXEC(N'ALTER DATABASE [Validation] SET READ_COMMITTED_SNAPSHOT ON;');
info: Microsoft.EntityFrameworkCore.Database.Command[200101]
      Executed DbCommand (8ms) [Parameters=[], CommandType='Text', CommandTimeout='30']
      CREATE TABLE [__EFMigrationsHistory] (
          [MigrationId] nvarchar(150) NOT NULL,
          [ProductVersion] nvarchar(32) NOT NULL,
          CONSTRAINT [PK___EFMigrationsHistory] PRIMARY KEY ([MigrationId])
      );
info: Microsoft.EntityFrameworkCore.Database.Command[200101]
      Executed DbCommand (4ms) [Parameters=[], CommandType='Text', CommandTimeout='30']
      SELECT OBJECT_ID(N'__EFMigrationsHistory');
info: Microsoft.EntityFrameworkCore.Database.Command[200101]
      Executed DbCommand (1ms) [Parameters=[], CommandType='Text', CommandTimeout='30']
      SELECT [MigrationId], [ProductVersion]
      FROM [__EFMigrationsHistory]
      ORDER BY [MigrationId];
info: Microsoft.EntityFrameworkCore.Migrations[200402]
      Applying migration '20170725021313_InitialMigration'.
Applying migration '20170725021313_InitialMigration'.
info: Microsoft.EntityFrameworkCore.Database.Command[200101]
      Executed DbCommand (2ms) [Parameters=[], CommandType='Text', CommandTimeout='30']
      CREATE TABLE [Employees] (
          [EmployeeId] int NOT NULL IDENTITY,
          [Designation] nvarchar(max) NULL,
          [Name] nvarchar(max) NULL,
          [Salary] decimal(18, 2) NOT NULL,
          CONSTRAINT [PK_Employees] PRIMARY KEY ([EmployeeId])
      );
info: Microsoft.EntityFrameworkCore.Database.Command[200101]
      Executed DbCommand (1ms) [Parameters=[], CommandType='Text', CommandTimeout='30']
      INSERT INTO [__EFMigrationsHistory] ([MigrationId], [ProductVersion])
      VALUES (N'20170725021313_InitialMigration', N'2.0.0-preview2-25794');
Done.
D:\...\Lesson4\MVCEF\MVCEF>
```

The following screenshot shows you the database created:

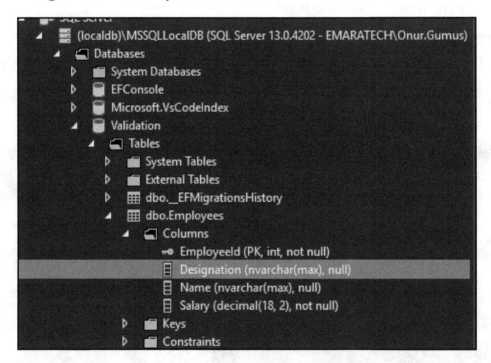

Run the application. You will get the following screen, where the user can enter the employee information in the form. As we are using the strongly typed model in our view, it takes the default values for all the properties. Name and Designation are properties of the string type and the default values are empty string for these fields, Salary is of the decimal type and the default value for decimal is 0, hence 0 is shown in the form when it is loaded for the Salary field.

As there are no records, we are showing 0 records in the `List of employees` table:

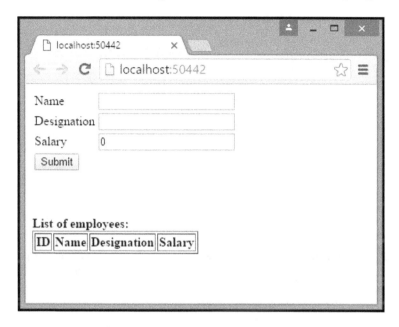

When you enter the information in the form and submit it, the information gets saved in the database and all the database records in the `Employees` table will be presented as follows:

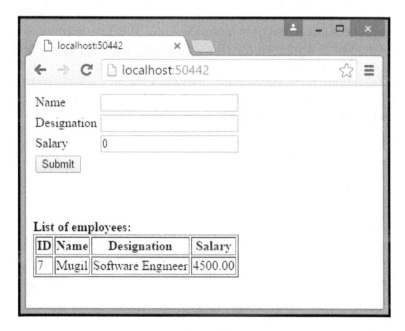

Adding an Age Property to the Employee Class and a New Migration

The `Employee` class will resemble this:

 Go to `https://goo.gl/2i6iRj` to access the code.

```
public class Employee
{
  public int EmployeeId { get; set; }
  public string Name { get; set; }
  public decimal Salary { get; set; }
  public string Designation { get; set; }
  public int Age { get; set; }
}
```

Then from the Package Manager Console, we run the `Add-Migration EmployeeAge` command.

Summary

In this chapter, we learned what a model is and how it fits in the ASP.NET MVC application. Then, we created a simple model, built model data in a controller, passed the model to the view, and showed the data using the view. We have learned about the models specific to a view and have discussed the flow of the data with respect to models. We learned about Entity Framework, an ORM framework from Microsoft, and how it simplifies database access from your .NET application. We have created a simple console application where we have inserted, updated, and deleted records. Finally, we have built an ASP.NET Core application that uses model, ViewModel, and Entity Framework.

5
Validation

We can never rely on the data entered by users. Sometimes they might be ignorant about the application and thus they may be entering incorrect data unknowingly. At other times, some malign users may want to corrupt the application by entering inappropriate data into it. In either case, we need to validate the input data before storing the data for further processing.

By the end of this chapter, you will be able to:

- Explain the different types of validation
- Perform server-side validation using an example
- Perform client-side validation using an example
- Perform unobtrusive JavaScript validation using jQuery unobtrusive libraries

Introduction to Validation

In an ideal case, users will enter valid data in a proper format in your application. But, as you might realize, the real world is not so ideal. Users will enter incorrect data in your application. As a developer, it is your responsibility to validate the user input in your application. If the entered input is not valid, you need to inform the user, explaining what has gone wrong, so that the user can correct the input data and submit the form again.

Validation can be done on the client side, on the server side, or at both ends. If the validation is done before sending the data to the server, it is called client-side validation. For example, if the user does not enter any data in a mandatory field, we can validate (by finding the data that is not entered) the form, at the client side itself.

There is no need to send the form data to the server. JavaScript is the most commonly-used language for client-side validation:

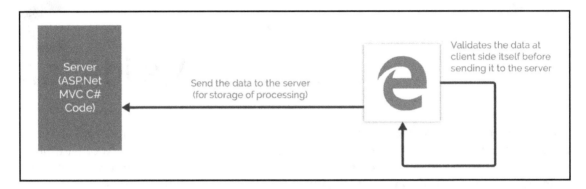

If the validation is done at the server side (sending the form data to the server), it is called server-side validation. For instance, you might want to validate data entered by the user against the data in the database. In this case, it is preferable to do server-side validation as we cannot have all the data in the database at the client side:

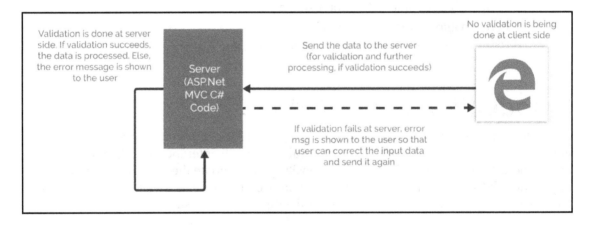

Server side validation is essential even if we don't use a database as you cannot trust the user. A malicious user can alter your data, HTML, or JavaScript in the browser and submit data that is actually incorrect. Server-side validation is your only real defense.

 Never trust client-side validation. For critical data, always do the validation on the server.

Client-Side and Server-Side Validation

In the real world, it's not a case of either server-side or client-side validation. Server-side validation is good for our own security. Client-side validation is convenient for the user. It also improves our performance. As the validation runs immediately within the user's browser, it doesn't have any impact on our server. We can have both types of validation at the same time. In fact, it is recommended to validate the data at both ends to avoid unnecessary processing:

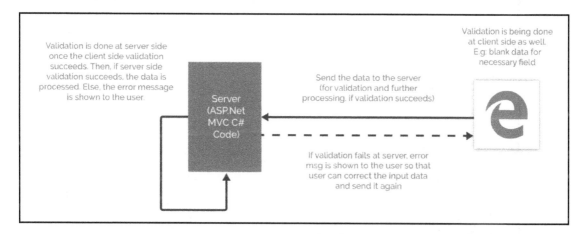

The preceding figure shows that the validation is being performed at both the client side and the server side. If the data is not entered into the required field, we can catch that issue at the client side itself. There is no need to send the data to the server to finally find out that there is no data entered. Once all the required data is entered, the data is sent back to the server to validate the entered data based on some business logic. If the validation fails, the form data is sent again to the browser with an error message so that the user can send the data again.

We have covered enough theory about the need for validation and the types of validations typically used in the application. Let's get our hands dirty by adding validation to the application that we built in the previous chapter.

The following screenshot is the form that we built in the previous chapter. There is nothing fancy in this form—just three fields.

When a user enters the data in the form, the data is stored in the database and all the employee information is fetched back and shown in a tabular format:

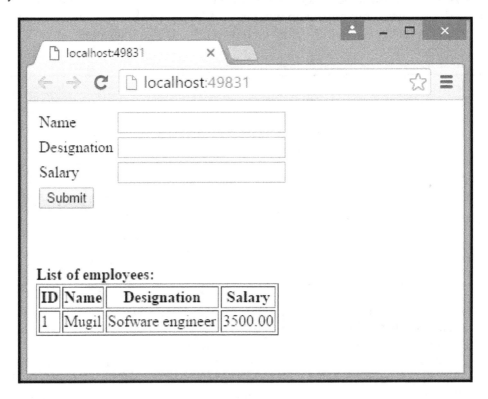

In the existing application that we built, we do not show any message to the user, even when the user does not enter any information in any of the fields and submits it. Instead, we silently store the default values for the fields (empty values for string types and 0.00 for decimal types), as shown in the following screenshot:

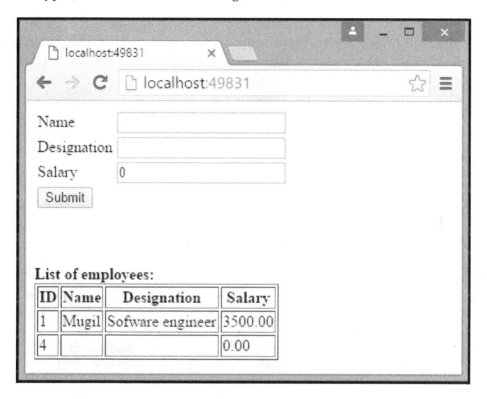

But this should not be the case. We should inform the user that the data entered is not valid and ask the user to correct the input data.

Server-Side Validation

Let's continue with the application that we built in the previous chapter. To perform a server-side validation, we need to do the following:

1. Add Data Annotation attributes to the `ViewModels` model class. The input data is validated against this metadata and the model state is updated automatically.
2. Update the `view` method to display the validation message for each of the fields. The `span` tag helper with the `asp-validation-for` attribute will be used to display the validation error message.
3. Update the controller action method to verify the model state. If the model state is valid, we insert the data into the database. Otherwise, the ViewModel is updated and the `view` method is rendered again with the validation error message so that the user can update with valid input data and submit the form again.

Updating ViewModels with the Data Annotation Attribute

The Data Annotation attribute defines the validation rules for the properties of the `Model/ViewModel`. If the input data does not match the attribute definition in the model, the validation will fail, which in turn makes the associated model state invalid. The reason for adding annotations to ViewModels is that we expose ViewModels to the outside world, not the models. Also, we don't want to pollute our business classes with ASP.NET-specific attributes.

There are several Data Annotation attributes available to validate the data. The following are the most commonly-used Data Annotation attributes:

- **Required**: This attribute indicates that the property is required.
- **Range**: This attribute defines the minimum and maximum constraints.
- **MinLength**: This defines the minimum length a property must have in order for the validation to succeed.
- **MaxLength**: As the name implies, this attribute defines the maximum length of the property. If the length of the property value exceeds the maximum length, the validation will fail.
- **RegularExpression**: We can use a regular expression for data validation if we use this attribute.

As Data Annotation attributes are available in the
`System.ComponentModel.DataAnnotations` namespace, we need to include this
namespace. The following is the updated ViewModel code from `Chapter 4`, *Models*:

 Go to `https://goo.gl/EgT2vC` to access the code.

```
using MVCEF.Models;
using System;
using System.Collections.Generic;
using System.ComponentModel.DataAnnotations;
using System.Linq;
using System.Threading.Tasks;
namespace MVCEF.ViewModels
{
    public class EmployeeAddViewModel
    {
        public List<Employee> EmployeesList { get; set; }
        [Required(ErrorMessage = "Employee Name is required")]
        public string Name { get; set; }
        [Required(ErrorMessage = "Employee Designation is required")]
        [MinLength(5, ErrorMessage = "Minimum length of designation should be 5
characters")]
        public string Designation { get; set; }
        [Required]
        [Range(1000, 9999.99)]
        public decimal Salary { get; set; }
    }
}
```

We have added Data Annotation attributes for all the three properties: `Name`,
`Designation`, and `Salary`.

The `ErrorMessage` attribute displays a message that will be displayed when the validation
fails. If there is a failure of validation and if there is no `ErrorMessage` mentioned, the
default error message will be displayed.

The drawbacks of using attributes is that it can only handle literals that are available at
compile time. If we need more dynamic validation, we can derive from
`ValidationAttribute` and add our own logic. Also, it is possible to use resource files to
localize the items.

Updating the ViewModel to Display the Validation Error Message

For each of the fields, we have added a span tag where the error message is displayed in a red color when the validation fails. When the validation succeeds, there will be no error message displayed. The attribute value of `asp-validation-for` represents the field name for which the validation error message has to be displayed. For example, we have used the span tag with the `asp-validation-for` attribute and with the `Name` value, which tells ASP.NET MVC to display the validation error message for the `Name` field.

`Views/Employee/Index.cshtml` looks as follows:

Go to `https://goo.gl/k9JMRf` to access the code.

```
@model MVCEF.ViewModels.EmployeeAddViewModel
@*
  //For more information on enabling MVC for empty projects, visit http://
  go.microsoft.com/fwlink/?LinkID=397860
*@
@{
}
...
  <td>
    <span asp-validation-for="Name" style="color:red"></span>
  </td>
...
```

Make sure you have `Views\_ViewImports.cshtml` to enable tag helpers, as follows: `@addTagHelper *,`
`Microsoft.AspNetCore.Mvc.TagHelpers`

Updating the Controller Action Method to Verify the Model State

The model state is automatically updated based on the Data Annotation attribute specified on our ViewModel and the input data. We are verifying whether the model state is valid in the following `Index` method, which is a `POST` action method. If the model state is valid (when the validation succeeds), we save the entered data to the database. If the validation fails, then the `ModelState` is set to `invalid` automatically. Then, we would populate `ViewModel` with the entered data and render the `View` method again so that the user can correct the input data and re-submit the data:

 Go to `https://goo.gl/iQHZYS` to access the code.

```
[HttpPost]
public IActionResult Index(EmployeeAddViewModel employeeAddViewModel)
{
  if (ModelState.IsValid)
  {
...
...
  }
  employeeAddViewModel.EmployeesList =
  employeeDbContext.Employees.ToList();
  return View(employeeAddViewModel);
}
```

When you run the application after making the aforementioned changes and submit the form without entering the values, error messages will be displayed beside the fields, as shown in the following screenshot. Please note that, even in the case of a validation error, we display the employees' data in the following table, which is achieved by using the code block in the previous code snippet:

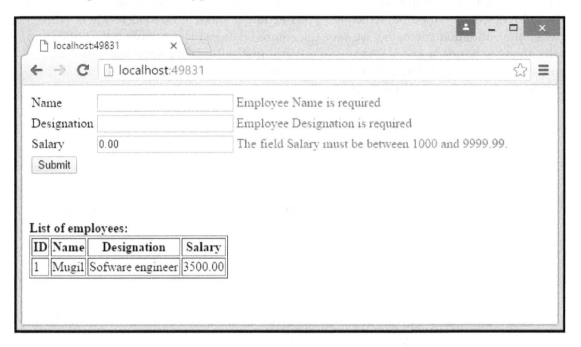

There are a few things to be noted in the previous validation and its error message:

- If the validation fails, error messages are displayed as expected.
- If there is more than one validation for the same field, it will display one error message at a time. For example, we have a couple of validations for the Designation field: the Required and MinLength attributes. If there is no data entered for the field, only the required field error message will be displayed. Only when the required field error is resolved (by entering some characters in the field), the second validation error message will be displayed.
- If no error message is available and if the validation fails, the default error message is displayed. We have not given an error message for the Salary field. So, when the validation fails for that field, ASP.NET MVC displays the default error message based on the field name and the type of validation failure.

It's not possible to circumvent the validation by editing the HTML code from the browser. The validation happens on the server side. It is safe and there is no way to work around it.

The following figure depicts the high-level sequence of events in server-side validation:

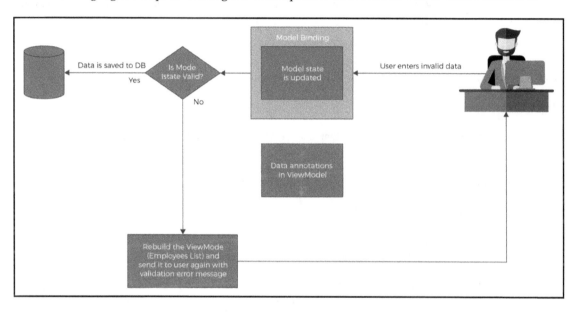

Here's the description of the preceding figure:

1. The user enters the invalid data.
2. Based on the Data Annotations attribute in the ViewModel, the model state is updated automatically. This happens during the model binding process where the data in the view method is mapped to the data in the model or ViewModel.
3. In the controller's action method, we are verifying the model state.
4. If the model state is valid, we are saving the entered data to the database.
5. If the model state is not valid, we are rending the ViewModel again with the validation error message so that the user can correct the input data and submit the form again with the valid input data.

Activity: Adding a New Validation Rule for Designation

Scenario

Your company wants you to add a new validation rule for designation so that it consists of at least two words. (Hint: use regex.)

Aim

Add a new validation rule for the designation property.

Steps for completion

Revise the `designation` property in `EmployeeAddViewModel.cs`, as follows:

Go to `https://goo.gl/bK5Ece` to access the code.

```
[Required(ErrorMessage = "Employee Designation is required")]
[MinLength(5, ErrorMessage = "Minimum length of designation should
be 5 characters")]
[RegularExpression(@"^[a-z]+(?:\s[a-z]+)+$", ErrorMessage =
"Designation should be at least two
words")]
public string Designation { get; set; }
```

Client-Side Validation

There are scenarios where we don't need to go to the server to validate the input data. In the preceding example of server-side validation, we do not need to go to the server to verify whether the user has entered the data for the `Name` field. We can validate at the client side itself. This prevents round-trips to the server and reduces the server load.

We are going to use JavaScript to validate the data from the client side. JavaScript is a high-level, interpreted language that is primarily used in client-side programming.

At present, JavaScript is also being used at the server side as part of Node.js.

Performing Client-Side Validation

Follow these steps to perform client-side validation:

1. We are going to make a couple of changes in our ViewModel (the `Index.cshtml` file) to validate the form at the client side:
   1. Changes in the form: add the `id` attribute to all the span tags so that we can access this HTML element to display the HTML error message. On submission of the form, call a JavaScript function to validate the input data.
   2. Add the script HTML element and create a JavaScript function to validate the input data.
2. In the following code, we are calling the `validateForm` JavaScript function on submission of the form. If the `validateForm` function returns `true`, the data will be sent to the server. Otherwise, the data will not be sent. We have added the `id` attribute for all the span tags so that we can identify the `span` tags and display the validation error messages over there:

 Go to `https://goo.gl/vjjtRp` to access the code.

```
<form asp-controller="Employee" asp-action="Index" onsubmit="return
validateForm()">
  <table>
    <tr>
      <td><label asp-for="Name"></label></td>
      <td><input asp-for="Name" /></td>
      <td>
      <span id="validationName" asp-validation-for="Name"
style="color:red"></span>
      </td>
    </tr>
...
...
    </tr>
  </table>
</form>
```

The purpose of `onsubmit="return validateForm()"` function is that returns false due to a validation error, then it will prevent the form from getting submitted to the server. Do not forget the return keyword, otherwise it won't work as expected.

3. We have added the JavaScript function to validate all three fields. We get the values of the three fields and store them in separate variables. Then we verify whether the value of each of the variables is null or empty. If the value is empty, we get the span element for the respective field and set the text context with the validation error message:

Go to `https://goo.gl/3uPtH1` to access the code.

```
<script type="text/javascript">
  function validateForm()
  {
    var isValidForm = true;
    var nameValue = document.getElementById("Name").value;
    var designationValue =
document.getElementById("Designation").value;
    var salaryValue = document.getElementById("Salary").value;
...
...
  }
</script>
```

4. When you run the application, and submit the form without entering the data, you'll get the error message generated from the client side itself without ever going to the server:

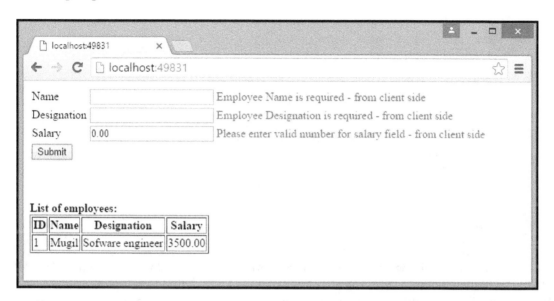

In real-world applications, we would not be hand coding the validation code on the JavaScript. Instead, most applications use unobtrusive validation, where we do not write JavaScript code for validating each of the fields. Simply adding the respective JavaScript libraries will do.

You might wonder how the fields get validated without ever writing the code. The magic lies in the `data-` attributes added to the input HTML elements based on the Data Annotation attributes. This jQuery unobtrusive library gets a list of fields for which `data-` attributes are added and it gets validated.

Run the application and press *Ctrl* + *U* to see the source code. The source code will look something like the following:

 Go to `https://goo.gl/gTYZKb` to access the code.

```
<div>
  <form action="/" method="post">
    <table>
      <tr>
        <td><label for="Name">Name</label></td>
        <td><input type="text" data-val="true" data-val-
required="Employee Name is required"
        id="Name" name="Name" value="" /></td>
  ...
  ...
    </form>
</div>
```

Different attributes will be added to different kinds of Data Annotation attributes. The data attributes were generated from the attributes that we have defined on top of our ViewModel. For the fields to be validated, the `data-val` attribute would be set to `true`. For the properties, which are marked as required in the ViewModel, the `data-val-required` attribute will have the value of the error message of the associated property.

Activity: Adding a New Validation Rule to a JavaScript Function

Aim

Add a new validation rule to the JavaScript function for designation so that it must consist of at least two words. (Hint: use regex.)

Steps for completion

We need to revise the JavaScript. Check the following:

Go to `https://goo.gl/u8y4Ur` to access the code.

```
//validate the designation field
if (designationValue == null || designationValue == "" )
{
  document.getElementById("validationDesignation").textContent =
  "Employee Designation is required - from
  client side";
isValidForm = false;
}
else if (!(/^[a-z]+(?:\s[a-z]+)+$/.test(designationValue )))
{
  document.getElementById(
"validationDesignation").textContent =
  "Employee Designation must be at least two
  words - from client side";
isValidForm = false;
}
```

Implementation

The layout file (_Layout.cshtml) defines the layout structure of your web application. As JavaScript libraries are going to be used in all the pages, this is the right place to add common functionalities such as unobtrusive validation.

Just add the JavaScript libraries (highlighted in bold in the following code snippet) to the layout file (_Layout.cshtml) so that they will be available for all the View files:

 Go to `https://goo.gl/MKJ39B` to access the code.

```
<!DOCTYPE html>
<html>
<head>
  <meta name="viewport" content="width=device-width" />
  <title>@ViewBag.Title</title>
</head>
<body>
  <div>
```

```
    @RenderBody()
  </div>
  <script
src="http://ajax.aspnetcdn.com/ajax/jQuery/jquery-2.2.3.js"></script>
  <script src="https://ajax.aspnetcdn.com/ajax/jquery.validate/
1.14.0/jquery.validate.min.js">  </script>
  <script
src="https://ajax.aspnetcdn.com/ajax/mvc/5.2.3/jquery.validate.unobtrusive.
min.js"></script>
</body>
</html>
```

There is no change to `ViewModel` except for the removal of the JavaScript function we wrote earlier for validating the fields. The complete code for the view is as follows:

 Go to `https://goo.gl/pxazJH` to access the code.

```
@model MVCEF.ViewModels.EmployeeAddViewModel
@*
//For more information on enabling MVC for empty projects, visit http://go.
microsoft.com/fwlink/?LinkID=397860
*@
@{
}
...
...
  </table>
</div>
```

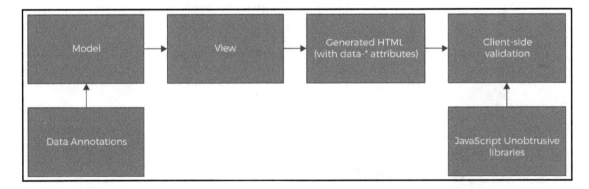

The preceding diagram depicts the unobtrusive client validation process:

1. Data Annotations are added to `Model/ViewModels`.
2. The view takes `Model/ViewModels` and generates the HTML.
3. The generated HTML from the ViewModel contains `data-*` attributes:
   - For the fields for which the `Required` attribute is set, the `data-val-required` attribute is created with the error message as its value.
   - For the fields with the `MinLength` Data Annotation attribute, the `data-val-minlength` attribute is set with the error message as its value.
   - For the range, Data Annotation, the `data-val-range` attribute is set with the error message as its value. The `data-val-range-max` represents the maximum value in the range and the `data-val-range-min` attribute represents the minimum value in the range.
4. The jQuery unobtrusive validation library reads these elements with `data-*` attributes and does the client-side validation. This means the developer does not have to write the separation validation code using JavaScript as everything is resolved by the configuration itself.

The data-val attributes are only generated from our pre-defined data attributes. If we had a complex custom logic and if we need them to validate from the client side, then we need to go back to write JavaScript.

Activity: Adding a New Validation Rule for Designation by Extending ValidationAttribute

Aim

Add a new validation rule for designation so that it must consist of at least two words. But this time do not use regex on server side. Instead, extend `ValidationAttribute`.

Steps for completion

1. Create the validator attribute, as follows:

 Go to `https://goo.gl/m63jKP` to access the code.

```
public class TwoWordsValidationAttribute : ValidationAttribute,
IClientModelValidator
{
  public void AddValidation(ClientModelValidationContext context)
...
...
}
```

2. Note that by using client model validator we also interact with the jQuery unobtrusive validation framework. Then put the following code in the Layout file at the bottom of the page:

 Go to `https://goo.gl/Px3d12` to access the code.

```
...
<script type="text/javascript">
$(function () {
jQuery.validator.addMethod('twowords', function (value, element,
params)
{
  var value = $(params[0]).val();
  return /^[a-z]+(?:\s[a-z]+)+$/.test(value);
});
...
...
  </script>
</body>
</html>
```

Summary

In this chapter, we learned about the need for validation and the different kinds of validation available. We have even discussed how client-side and server-side validation work, along with the pros and cons of each type of validation. Later, we made code changes to validate the input data at the server side. Then we used JavaScript to validate the input data in the client side itself. Finally, we used the jQuery unobtrusive library to do the client-side validation without ever writing the JavaScript code to validate the input data at the client side.

In the next chapter, we will discuss the routing principle and how to customize it. In an earlier chapter, we saw the basics of routing in an ASP.NET 5 application. Now we are going to explore this topic in depth.

6
Routing

Routing is one of the most important concepts in the ASP.NET MVC application as it takes care of incoming requests and maps them to the appropriate controller's actions.

We briefly discussed routing in `Chapter 2`, *Controllers*. In this chapter, we are going to discuss routing along with several options available for customizing it in ASP.NET Core.

By the end of this chapter, you will be able to:

- Use the MapRoute method to configure routing
- Work with different types of routing with examples—convention and attribute-based
- Use HTTP verbs in attribute-based routing

Convention-Based Routing

The routing engine is responsible for mapping the incoming requests to the appropriate action method of the controller.

We should have route names as it gives the route a logical name so that the named route can be used for URL generation. This greatly simplifies URL creation when the ordering of routes could make URL generation complicated. Routes names must be unique application-wide.

Route names have no impact on URL matching or handling of requests; they are used only for URL generation. Though URL generation is a different topic to study, we can say briefly that we use it for generating links from one page to another in our views.

In the `Configure` method of the `Startup` class, we have mapped the following route:

```
app.UseMvc(routes =>
{
   routes.MapRoute(
      name: "default",
      template: "{controller=Employee}/{action=Index}/{id?}");
});
```

Alternatively, you can use the following code:
`app.UseMvcWithDefaultRoute();`
This is equal to the following:
```
app.UseMvc(routes =>
{
   routes.MapRoute(
      name: "default",
      template: "{controller=Home}/{action=Index}/{id?}");
});
```

The `MapRoute` method has two parameters:

- `name`: This represents the name of the route as we could configure multiple routes for the same application.
- `template`: This signifies the actual configuration for the route. There are three parts to this configuration value. As we are supplying default parameters, if the values are not passed, it will take the default parameter values.
  - `{controller=Employee}`: The first value acts as the name of the controller. We use the Employee controller as the default controller when the controller value is not available in the URL.
  - `{action=Index}`: The `Index` action method will be acting as the default action method. The second parameter from the URL will be taken as the action method name.
  - `{id?}`: By specifying "?" after the id parameter, we are saying that id is the optional parameter. If the value is passed as the third parameter, the `id` value will be taken. Otherwise, it would not be considered.

Let us see a few examples and observe how our routing engine works. We are assuming the following routing for the preceding examples:

```
"{controller=Employee}/{action=Index}/{id?}"
```

Example 1

This is how the URL appears:

http://localhost:49831/

In this URL, we have not passed a value for the `controller`, `action`, or `id` parameters. Since we have not passed anything, it would take the default values for the controller and the action. So, the URL is converted into the following URL by the routing engine:

http://localhost:49831/Employee/Index

Example 2

This is how the URL appears:

http://localhost:49831/Employee/

In this URL, we have passed the value for the controller (the first parameter), which is `Employee`, whereas we did not pass anything for the `action` method (the second parameter) or `id` (the third parameter). So, the URL will be converted into the following URL, taking the default value for the `action` method:

http://localhost:49831/Employee/Index

Example 3

This is how the URL appears:

http://localhost:49831/Manager/List

The routing engine will take the first parameter, Manager, as the controller name and the second parameter, List, as the action method name.

Example 4

This is how the URL appears:

http://localhost:49831/Manager/Details/2

We have passed all three parameters in this URL. So, the first parameter value, Manager, will be considered as the controller method name. The second parameter value will be considered as the action method name. The third parameter value will be considered as the id.

When defining the map route, we use the MapRoute method with a couple of parameters. The first parameter, name, represents the name of the route and the second parameter, template, represents the URL pattern to be matched along with the default values. Here's some sample code for your observation:

```
routes.MapRoute(name: "default",
  template:
  "{controller=Employee}/{action=Index}/{id?}");
```

There are other overloaded variations of this MapRoute method. The following is another commonly overloaded MapRoute method, where the incoming URL pattern and the default values are passed for different parameters. The name of the route is FirstRoute and this route will be applied for all URLs starting with Home. The default values for the controller and the action are Home and Index2, respectively, as shown here:

```
routes.MapRoute(name: "FirstRoute",
  template: "Home",
  defaults: new { controller = "Home", action = "Index2" });
```

You can define any number of routing maps for your ASP.NET MVC application. There is no restriction or limit on the routing maps. Let's add another routing map to our application. We have added another route map called FirstRoute to our application:

 Go to https://goo.gl/36qj7c to access the code.

```
public void Configure(IApplicationBuilder app, IHostingEnvironment env)
{
    app.UseMvc(routes =>
    {
        routes.MapRoute(name: "FirstRoute",
        template: "Home", defaults: new
        {
            controller = "Home",
            action = "Index2"
        });
        routes.MapRoute(name: "default",
        template:
        "{controller=Employee}/{action=Index}/{id?}");
    });
}
```

And we have added another controller method by the name of `HomeController` with a couple of simple action methods that return different strings:

Go to `https://goo.gl/avdJM9` to access the code.

```
public class HomeController : Controller
{
    // GET: /<controller>/
    public IActionResult Index()
    {
        return Content("Index action method");
    }
    public IActionResult Index2()
    {
        return Content("Index2 action method");
    }
}
```

When you try to access the application through the URL, `http://localhost:49831/Hello`, both routing maps, `FirstRoute` and the default, match with the URL pattern.

The routing engine maps the incoming URL based on the following factors:

- The matching pattern
- The order defined in the routing engine

The first factor is an obvious one. For a routing map to be picked up by the routing engine, the pattern of the incoming URL should get matched with the defined template in the routing map.

The second factor is subtle but important. If more than one routing map matches with the incoming URL, the routing engine will pick the first URL as defined in the configuration.

For example, if the incoming URL matches with both the `FirstRoute` and `default` maps, the routing engine will pick the `FirstRoute` map as it was defined first in the configuration:

If the routing engine could not map the incoming URL to any of the mapping routes, we get an `HTTP 404 error`, meaning that no resource could be found. You can see the status (**200** means **OK**, **404** means **No resource found**) by looking at the **Network** tab in the developer tools, as shown in the following screenshot:

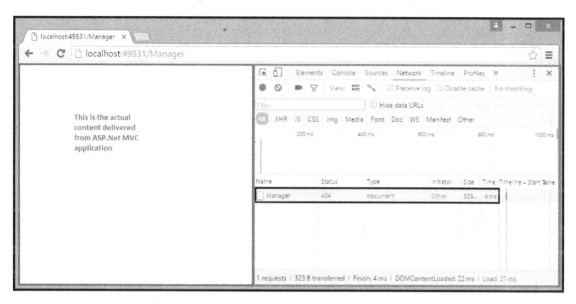

Attribute-Based Routing

Until now, we have used convention-based routing. In convention-based routing, we define the routing templates (which are just parameterized strings) in a centralized place that is applicable to all the available controllers. The problem with convention–based routing is that, if we want to define different URL patterns for different controllers, we need to define a custom URL pattern that is common to all the controllers. Also, convention-based routing sets our general routing template. It is more flexible; changing it programmatically at runtime is possible. This makes things difficult.

There is another option for configuring the attribute-based engine routing. In attribute-based routing, instead of configuring all the routing in a centralized location, the configuration will happen at the controller level. We can customize and override our conventions. Attribute-based routing is more static and determined at runtime.

Working on an Example of Attribute-Based Routing

Follow these steps to explore attribute-based routing:

1. First, let us remove the convention-based routing that we created earlier in the Configure method in the startup.cs class file:

```
public void Configure(IApplicationBuilder app,
IHostingEnvironment env)
{
  app.UseMvc();
  //app.UseMvc(routes =>
  //{
  //    routes.MapRoute(name: "FirstRoute",
  //    template: "Home", defaults: new
  //    {
  //      controller = "Home",
  //      action = "Index2"
  //    });
  //    routes.MapRoute(name: "default",
  //    template:
  "{controller=Employee}/{action=Index}/{id?}");
  //});
}
```

2. Then, we can configure the routing at the controller itself. In the following code, we have added the routing configuration for the home controller that we created earlier:

```
public class HomeController : Controller
{
  // GET: /<controller>/
  [Route("Home")]
  public IActionResult Index()
  {
    return Content("Index action method");
  }
  [Route("Home/Index3")]
  public IActionResult Index2()
  {
    return Content("Index2 action method");
  }
}
```

We have used the Route attribute in the `action` methods of the controller. The value passed in the Route `attribute` will be acting as the URL pattern. For example, when we access the `http://localhost:49831/Home/` URL, the Index method of `HomeController` will be called. When we access the `http://localhost:49831/Home/Index3` URL, the `Index2` method of `HomeController` will be called.

 The URL pattern and `action` method name do not need to match.

In the preceding example, we are calling the `Index2` action method, but the URL pattern uses `Index3`, `http://localhost:49831/Home/Index3`.

When you use attribute-based routing and convention-based routing together, attribute-based routing will take precedence.

Route Attribute at the Controller Level

You will notice that, with the URL pattern for the `action` methods, `Index` and `Index2`, we repeat the controller name, `Home`, in both URL patterns, `Home` and `Home/Index3`. Instead of repeating the `controller` method name (or any common part in the URL) at the `action` method level, we can define it at the controller level.

In the following code, the common part of the URL (Home) is defined at the controller level and the unique part is defined at the `action` method level. When the URL pattern is getting mapped to the `action` methods of the controller, both route parts (at the `controller` level and at the `action` method level) are merged and matched. So, there will be no difference between the routes defined earlier and those that follow.

If you want any parameters in attribute-based routing, you can pass them within curly brackets. In the following example, we did this for the `SayHello` action method.

For example, the `http://localhost:49831/Home/Index3` URL pattern will still get mapped to the `Index2` method of the `Homecontroller`:

```
[Route("Home")]
public class HomeController : Controller
{
    // GET: /<controller>/
    [Route("")]
    public IActionResult Index()
```

```
    {
      return Content("Index action method");
    }
    [Route("Index3")]
    public IActionResult Index2()
    {
      return Content("Index2 action method");
    }
    [Route("SayHello/{id}")]
    public IActionResult SayHello(int id)"
    {
      return Content("Say Hello action method" + id);
    }
}
```

Token Replacement in Route Templates

If you want your route to be based on the class and action names and still want to use attributes, there is a middle way of using attributes for conventional routing: token replacement.

[action], [area], and [controller] will be replaced with the values of the action name, area name, and controller name from the action where the route is defined. Let's see an example. Here is the original code:

```
[Route("[controller]/[action]")]
public class ProductsController : Controller
  {
  [HttpGet] // Matches '/Products/List'
  public IActionResult List()
  {
    // ...
  }
  [HttpGet("{id}")] // Matches '/Products/Edit/{id}'
  public IActionResult Edit(int id)
  {
    // ...
  }
}
```

The following code shows the change:

```
public class ProductsController : Controller
{
  [HttpGet("[controller]/[action]")] // Matches '/Products/List'
  public IActionResult List()
```

```
  {
    // ...
  }
  [HttpGet("[controller]/[action]/{id}")] // Matches '/Products/Edit/{id}'
  public IActionResult Edit(int id)
  {
    // ...
  }
}
```

Attribute routes can also be combined with inheritance. This is particularly powerful combined with token replacement:

```
[Route("api/[controller]")]
public abstract class MyBaseController : Controller { ... }
public class ProductsController : MyBaseController
{
  [HttpGet] // Matches '/api/Products'
  public IActionResult List() { ... }
  [HttpPost("{id}")] // Matches '/api/Products/{id}'
  public IActionResult Edit(int id) { ... }
}
```

Activity: Combining Route Templates that Begin with /

Scenario

Route templates applied to an action that begin with a / do not get combined with route templates applied to the controller. This example matches a set of URL paths similar to the *default route*. Based on this information, revise SayHello so that we can access it by writing http://localhost:<yourport>/Employee/SayHello/1.

Aim

Solve the issue of combining route templates that begin with / with route templates applied to the controller.

Steps for completion

Use the following code:

 Go to `https://goo.gl/q97bvZ` to access the code.

```
[Route("/Employee/SayHello/{id}")]
public IActionResult SayHello(int id)
{
  return Content("Say Hello action method" + id);
}
```

The following code shows the use of multiple routes:

```
[Route("Store")]
[Route("[controller]")]
public class ProductsController : Controller
{
  [HttpPost("Buy")] // Matches 'Products/Buy' and 'Store/Buy'
  [HttpPost("Checkout")] // Matches 'Products/Checkout' and
'Store/Checkout'
  public IActionResult Buy()
}
```

Passing Routing Values in HTTP Action Verbs in the Controller

Instead of passing the routing values as Route attributes, we can pass the routing values in HTTP action verbs, such as `HTTPGet` and `HTTPPost`.

In the following code, we have used the `HTTPGet` attribute to pass the route values. For the `Index` method, we did not pass any value and hence no route value will get appended to the route value defined at the `controller` method level. For the `Index2` method, we are passing the `Index3` value. `Index3` will get appended to the route value defined at the `controller` level. Please note that only URLs with GET methods will be mapped to the `action` methods. If you access the same URL pattern with the `POST` method, these routes will not get matched and hence these `action` methods will not get called:

```
[Route("Home")]
public class HomeController : Controller
```

```
{
  // GET: /<controller>/
  [HttpGet()]
  public IActionResult Index()
  {
    return Content("Index action method");
  }
  [HttpGet("Index3")]
  public IActionResult Index2()
  {
    return Content("Index2 action method");
  }
}
```

Activity: Defining Two Actions with the Same Name with Different Verbs

Scenario

You're tasked to define two actions with the same name with different verbs such as POST and GET. How will you do it so that you're more RESTful with the controllers?

Aim

Define two actions having the same names with different verbs, such as POST and GET.

Steps for completion

Use the following code:

 Go to https://goo.gl/nxs7tK to access the code.

```
[Route("Home")]
public class HomeController : Controller
{
  // GET: /<controller>/
  [HttpGet()]
  public IActionResult Index()
  {
    return Content("Index action method");
  }
  [HttpGet("Index3")]
```

```
      public IActionResult Index2()
      {
        return Content("Index2 action method");
      }
      [HttpPost("Index3")]
      public IActionResult Index2_Post()
      {
        return Content("Index2 post method");
      }
  }
```

See the Fiddler output as follows:

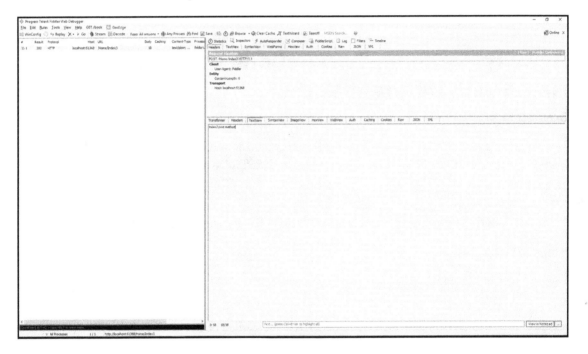

Route Constraints

Route Constraints enable you to constrain the type of values that you pass to the controller action. It is all about action selection for routing. So, we can say one action should trigger for integer input whereas another should trigger for non-integers. For example, if you want to restrict the value to be passed to the int type, you can do so. The following is one such instance:

```
[HttpGet("details2/{id:int}")]
  public IActionResult Details2(int id = 123)
  {
    return View();
  }
```

ASP.NET Core even supports default parameter values so that you can pass the default parameters:

```
[HttpGet("details2/{id:int}")]
  public IActionResult Details2(int id = 123)
  {
    return View();
  }
```

There are many constraints available, such as `int` and `bool`.

Activity: Creating an Attribute that Implements IActionConstraintFactory

Scenario

By using `IActionConstraint` and `IActionConstraintFactory` interfaces we can add custom constraints. Create an attribute that implements `IActionConstraintFactory` and returns an `IActionConstraint`. Use it and modify the below code so that for the `Accept: text/html` header, Index2_HTML is called but for `Accept: application/json`, Index2_Json is called. You may use Fiddler to send the requests.

```
[Route("Home")]
public class HomeController : Controller
{
  // GET: /<controller>/
  [HttpGet()]
  public IActionResult Index()
  {
    return Content("Index action method");
  }
  [HttpGet("Index2")]
  public IActionResult Index2_HTML()
  {
    return Content("HTML response returns");
  }
  [HttpGet("Index2")]
  public IActionResult Index2_JSON()
```

```
    {
      return Content("Json response returns");
    }
  }
```

Aim

To create an attribute that implements `IActionConstraintFactory` and returns an `IActionConstraint`

Steps for completion

1. We first create `AcceptHeaderActionConstraint` as follows:

 Go to `https://goo.gl/nUvECW` to access the code.

```
public class AcceptHeaderActionConstraint : IActionConstraint
{
  readonly string headerValue;
  public AcceptHeaderActionConstraint(string headerValue)
  {
    this.headerValue = headerValue;
  }
  public int Order => 0;
  public bool Accept(ActionConstraintContext context)
  {
    var headerVal = context.RouteContext.
    HttpContext.Request.Headers["Accept"];
    return headerVal.Contains(this.headerValue);
  }
}
```

2. Then, we create our actions, as follows:

 Go to `https://goo.gl/HdMzjq` to access the code.

```
public class AcceptHeaderAttribute : Attribute,
IActionConstraintFactory
{
  readonly string value;
  public AcceptHeaderAttribute(string value)
```

```
  => this.value = value;
  public bool IsReusable => true;
  public IActionConstraint CreateInstance(IServiceProvider
services)
  => new AcceptHeaderActionConstraint(this.value);
}
```

3. And decorate our actions, as follows:

 Go to https://goo.gl/dK9ZJ1 to access the code.

```
[Route("Home")]
public class HomeController : Controller
{
  // GET: /<controller>/
  [HttpGet()]
  public IActionResult Index()
  {
    return Content("Index action method");
  }
  [AcceptHeader("text/html")]
  [HttpGet("Index2")]
  public IActionResult Index2_HTML()
  {
    return Content("HTML response returns");
  }
  [AcceptHeader("application/json")]
  [HttpGet("Index2")]
  public IActionResult Index2_JSON()
  {
    return Content("Json response returns");
  }
}
```

The output for a sample request will be as follows:

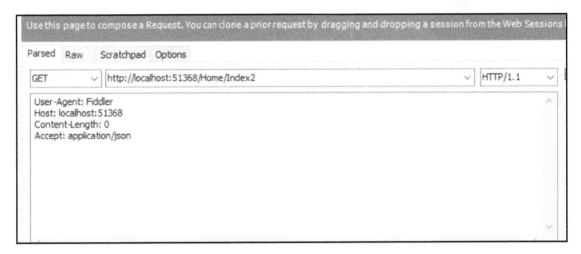

Note that for the sake of simplicity we are just returning arbitrary strings. In a real application we would have returned real objects.

Summary

In this chapter, we have learned about routing and how it works. We learned about the different kinds of routing available. We discussed convention-based routing and attribute-based routing with different examples. We also discussed route constraints and the default parameter values that could be passed.

In the next chapter, we'll start building our Rest Buy application.

7
Rest Buy

Routing is one of the most important concepts in the ASP.NET MVC application, as it takes care of incoming requests and maps them to the appropriate controller's actions.

In this chapter, we will try to apply what we have learned and start building a simplified real-world application. We will begin the development of a simple shopping cart application called **Rest Buy**. We call it Rest Buy because we will also try to employ RESTful tactics during the development.

In the Rest Buy project, we will make use of ASP.NET Core MVC along with Entity Framework and SQL Server, since this is the topic of the book, and try to employ a RESTful strategy. You will have a better idea about what we mean by RESTful through the development.

Note that these days, **Single-Page Applications (SPA)** are quite popular. There are lots of job opportunities for developers who work on frameworks such as Angular and React (used for Single-Page Applications). And these applications go to such extents as to turn an entire page into one single HTML document. This has some significant advantages as client-side developers can work almost completely isolated from the server side, and they develop the UI as if they are developing any mobile application. Also, they can isolate themselves from the tech stack that is used in the server. In addition to that, Visual Studio 2017 now also has Single-Page Application templates that you can use. However, in this course we will not build a Single-Page Application as we think this approach has also some potential drawbacks—or at least, can be slightly uncomfortable at times.

In the SPA approach, we usually load the HTML page without any data at first. Later, the data is loaded with a secondary AJAX request. This may require, at least for the very first time, your application to have some sort of initial loading screen. Such loading screens are tolerable in mobile apps. However, when it is about web applications your visitors will not desire to wait even for a few seconds.

Secondly, although search engines these days can render JavaScript, search engine optimization can still be tricky with the SPA approach.

Thirdly, there can be some discrepancy in the routing mechanism because with SPAs you start to manage URL routing from JavaScript as well as server side. This duality can be cumbersome to deal with at times.

Finally, from a RESTful point of view we would like to think that once we hit a URL like `/Products`, and when we make use of the `text/html` accept header, our intent is get products' representations as HTML, but not just dummy SPA HTML, and then load the products there. We know that World Wide Web is a proven technology and the ideas behind it like Rest and Hypermedia are something we can trust.

Having said that, this doesn't mean we can ignore client state. We still need to make use of AJAX not just to improve the user experience but also because the browser is responsible for maintaining application state in its memory. (We could also resort to cookies and local storage but that would be a bit more difficult.)

To sum up, we decided to go with a hybrid approach. We will briefly use these SPA frameworks for a fragment of a page whenever they are needed but also stick to server-side rendering and routing in general. For some cases, some parts can be rendered initially from the server side and then from the client side. This is an opinionated approach and we suggest you stick to whatever approach works for you in your career.

By the end of this chapter, you will be able to:

- Design Rest Buy
- Create the entities for the application
- Create EF context and migrations

Designing Rest Buy

We will start developing a simple shopping cart application in an iterative fashion. The features, screens, and user stories will also be explained along the way. However, for the sake of simplicity, we will give you a basic skeleton or a framework to start with and you need to fill the remaining transaction. The purpose of this application is to glimpse how a real life application is done. We will assume the data, such as products, are entered into the database by some other means. In our case, we will either hand edit or use database migrations.

In this book, we'll cover the Registration feature in `Chapter 8`, *Adding Features, Testing, and Deployment*. As mentioned, we're following iterative building of the application. Hence, as and when the next features are developed and you wish to refer to them, you can find them here: `https://github.com/OnurGumus/Packt_ASPNET_Core_RestBuy`

Features and Stories

Let's define our user stories and features:

Feature	Story			
	Functionality 1	Functionality 2	Functionality 3	Functionality 4
List products	As a registered or unregistered customer, when you visit the home page it should show a list of products.	As a registered or unregistered customer in the product list page, when you click on a product it should show the product detail page.		
Search and filter products	As a registered or unregistered customer, you should be able to filter the products as per categories. A product can be associated with multiple categories. So, when you select one or more categories and click on Filter, a filter should be applied until the page changes.	As a registered or unregistered customer, you should be able to filter the products by a price range. Here, there will be a minimum and maximum price and when you select a range this should be applied along with a category filter.	As a registered or unregistered customer, when you write some text in the search textbox, it should filter the product's description and name.	

Show product details	As a registered or unregistered customer, you should be able to bookmark each product, which should be displayed with a unique URL.	As a registered or unregistered customer, when you visit a product page, it should show you the product's name, photo, description and price.		
Shopping Cart	As a registered or unregistered customer, you should be able to add or remove products to the shopping cart.	As a registered or unregistered customer, you should be able to utilize the checkout panel to view your current added items.	As a registered or unregistered customer, you should be able to go to checkout page by clicking on the checkout panel.	As a registered customer, you should be able to check out and confirm your cart to convert it to an order.
Manage Orders	As a registered customer, you should be able to view your order details.			
Login	As a registered customer, you should be able to log into the application.			
Logout	As a registered customer, you should be able to log out of the application.			

 From the agile point of view, features and stories are not hierarchical. Features are more like tags to the user stories. Still, for simplicity and clarification, it is shown as hierarchical.

Layout and Pages

After defining our features, a good way to design our application is UX. By UX we refer to the user experience. UX doesn't mean we should program or design our UI first. UX helps us to identify the possible flows of our application from a user point of view and they have to be supported and complemented by the features.

Main Page

The main page can look similar to what is shown in the following screenshot:

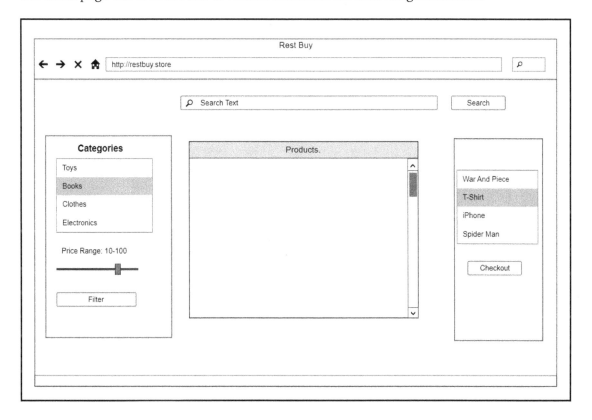

Product Detail

The **Product Detail** page can look similar to what is shown in the following screenshot:

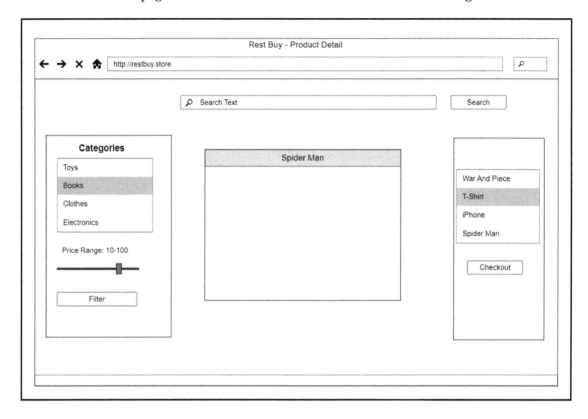

Checkout

The **Checkout** page can look similar to what is shown in the following screenshot:

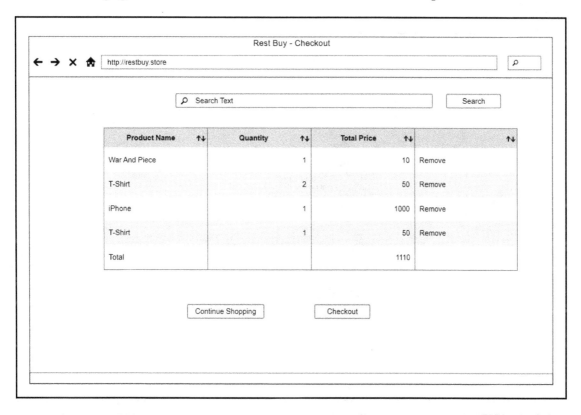

Checkout Success

The **Checkout Successful** page can look similar to what is shown in the following screenshot:

Previous Orders

The **Previous Orders** page can look similar to what is shown in the following screenshot:

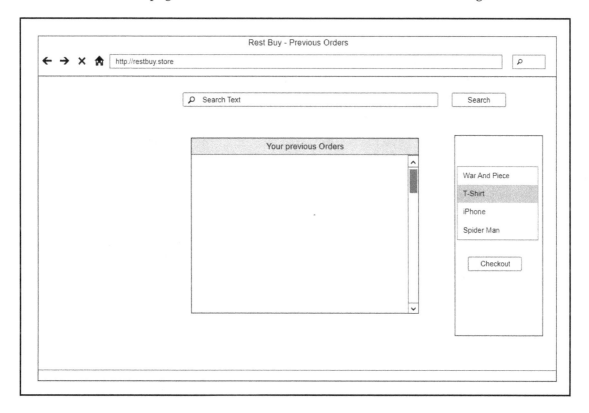

As you can see in some of the screenshots, we omitted the filter. It is an arbitrary decision; we thought that for the pages that we don't display products on, there is no point in keeping the filters, but still we have kept our search box at the top.

Defining our Domain and Model

The next thing is to define our model. Here we will try to apply domain-driven design. In domain-driven design, we model our classes based on the business domain and terminology. Obviously, if you have read the user stories, we already have a lot of clues about our domain, classes, and their properties.

For the time being, we can model our domain with 5 classes: Product, Order, User, OrderItem, and StockAmount. In this case, product and user are separate aggregates. An aggregate is a domain-driven development concept. Aggregates are used to designate independent parts of our domain classes. Typically, each aggregate consists of one or more classes and each represents a set of independent invariants. We have the following invariants:

- An order has at least 1 order item.
- An order has a create date and a user ID.
- An order item denotes a quantity and price and product ID.
- For an order item, quantity and price cannot be zero.
- An unconfirmed order denotes the current shopping cart.
- A customer can have maximum 1 unconfirmed order. (Drops to zero when checkout is completed)
- For an order item, the product ID must be valid. For a product, stock amount and price must be greater than or equal to zero.
- For StockAmount, the quantity must be equal to the quantity in an order item.

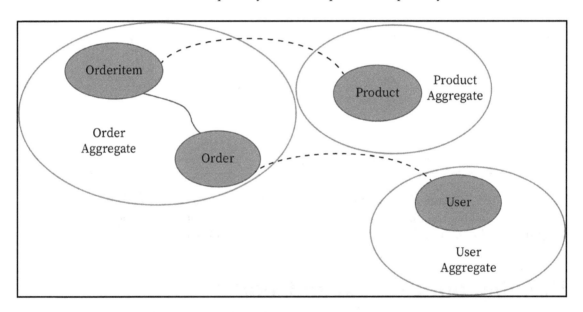

In the preceding diagram, we have defined three aggregates as **Order**, **Product**, and **User**. The dash lines above show indirect reference via the ID field whereas the solid line between **Order** and **OrderItem** refers to a direct reference. The very reason we have chosen this approach is that different modules of the application, such as the administration module, may want to deal with an aggregate independently. Changing a user's postal address should not affect the user's existing orders and order items. They are very much independent from each other. We can also move these entities to different micro services.

After all, our business invariants and constraints should only hold per an aggregate. Again, there is no absolute right way to do this, it depends on the project and how much you invest in future. As for the shopping cart itself, we will use the **Order** entity if the order is unconfirmed.

Creating a RestBuy Project

Having equipped ourselves with our initial design ideas, we can start implementing our project in practice. Follow these steps:

1. Create a new solution and Web Application as shown in the following screenshot. Make sure we name the project `RestBuy.Web`, and the solution name as `RestBuy`:

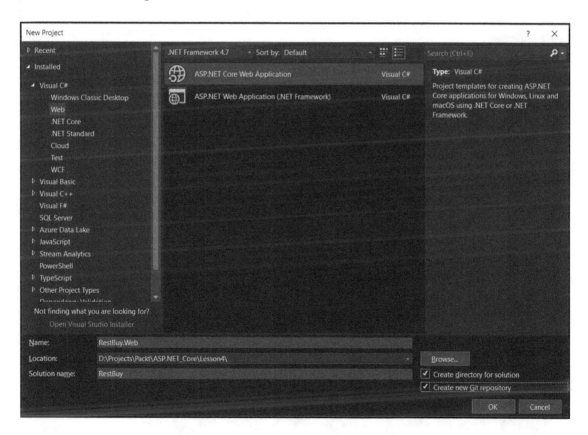

2. Select the MVC option and click on **OK**:

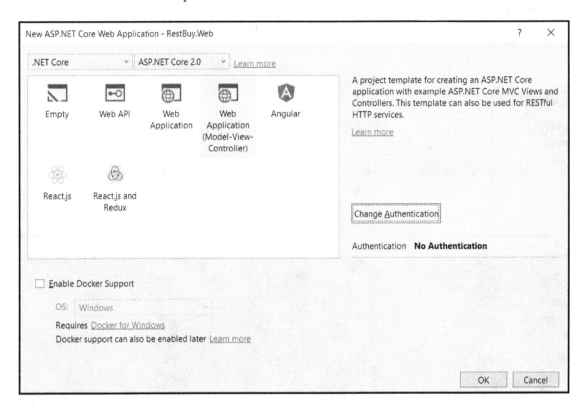

You'll see this:

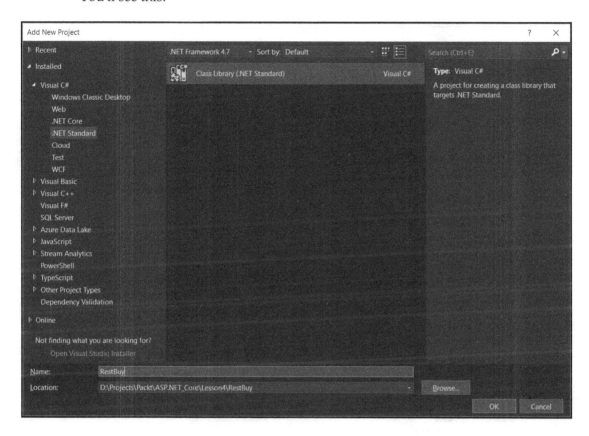

3. Add a new project as a .NET Standard Class Library called RestBuy:

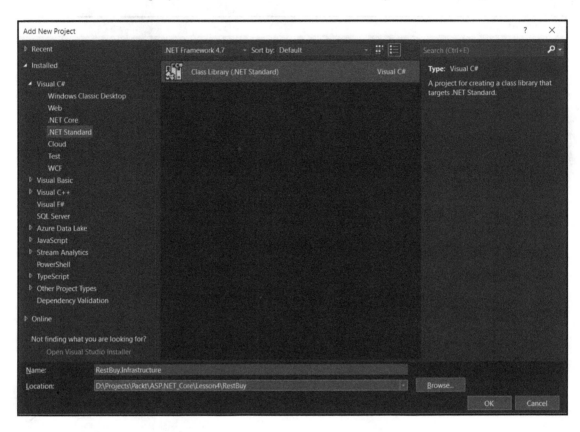

4. Add another Project as a .NET Standard Class Library called
`RestBuy.InfraStructure`:

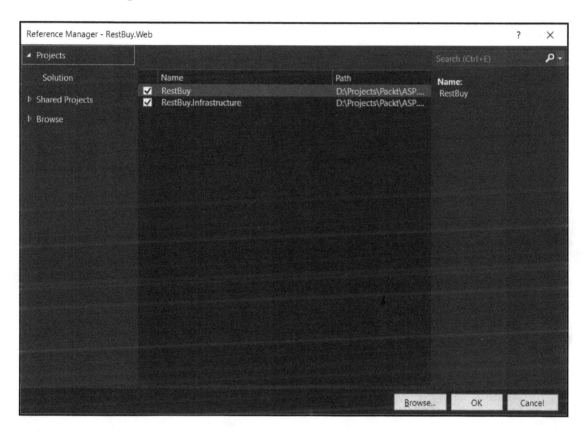

5. Right click on the dependencies section in the solution explorer for the `RestBuy.Web` project and add dependencies to the other projects:

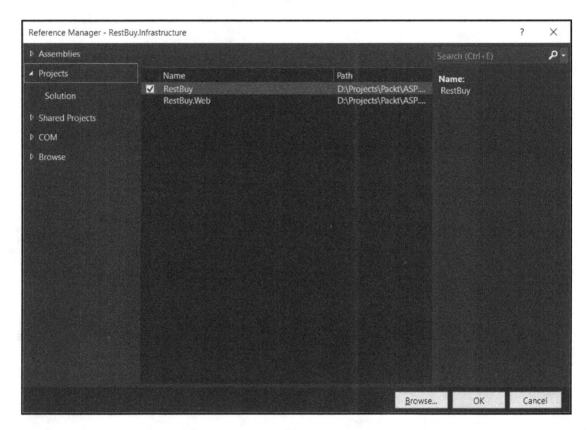

6. Similar to `RestBuy.InfraStructure`, add a reference to `RestBuy`.

 The `RestBuy` project itself references no other project.

Now, your project structure will look as follows:

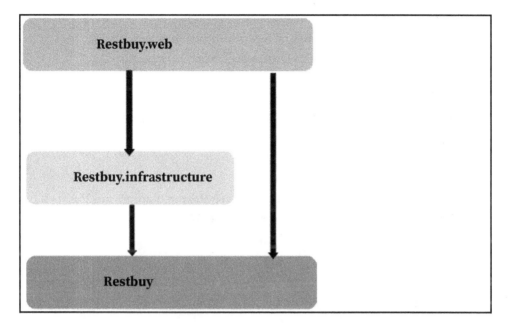

 In case our business logic is not aware of the database layer, we will put our database interfaces to the business layer and do their implementations in the infrastructure and use a dependency injection (not inversion) framework to inject those interfaces to retrieve data from the database. This is the dependency inversion principle.

Activity: Preparing Features and Stories for a Website

Scenario

Your client happens to be a fashion designer. He wants you to build a website for him. You need to first prepare features and stories for his website.

Aim

Prepare features and stories for a website.

Steps for completion

1. List down all the activities that a fashion designer does.
2. List down the web pages that he'll need for his business.
3. Write the features along with stories accompanying them.

Activity: Preparing Wireframe Diagrams for a Website

Scenario

Your client, the fashion designer, wants to see the wireframe diagrams of the web pages. You can prepare a wireframe diagram for the home page.

Aim

Prepare a wireframe diagram for a web page.

Steps for completion

1. Go to `https://www.draw.io/`.
2. In the Save diagrams to: dialog box, select Device.
3. In the Device dialog box, click on Create New Diagram.
4. In the next window, choose Basic (1), give a name to the file, and click on **Create**.
5. You'll be presented with the workspace screen, as shown in the following screenshot:

6. Click on the More Shapes button on the bottom left-hand corner of the screen (marked by a blue box in the preceding screenshot).
7. In the Shapes dialog box, select Mockups under the Software category. You can uncheck the rest of the options.
8. Click on Apply. You're ready to go.

Activity: Designing a Domain Model for a Website

Scenario

You want to design a domain model for the website you're building for your client, the fashion designer.

Aim

Design a domain model for a website.

Steps for completion

1. List down the classes you'll require to model your domain.
2. Define the aggregates.
3. Use draw.io to design a diagram and mention the aggregates and classes.
4. Use dashed lines to show indirect reference between the classes.
5. Use solid lines to show direct reference between the classes.

Creating the Entities

Now that we have our dependencies clarified, we can start creating our entities. You can delete existing `Class1.cs` files in the libraries.

Follow these steps to create the entities for Rest Buy:

1. Create an `Entities` folder in the `RestBuy` project as shown in the following screenshot:

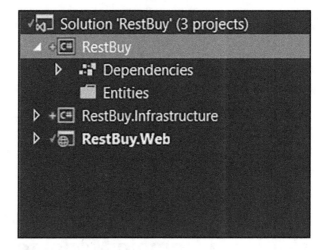

2. Inside the `Entities` folder we need to create four classes:
   * `BaseEntity`: This is the base class for all our entities
   * `Order`: This class will contain the logic behind the ordering of products.
   * `OrderItem`: This class is for containing order details.
   * `Product`: This class is for containing details of the products.
   * `StockAmount`: This class represents how many products are left in the store of a type.

3. Have this code inside `BaseEntity`:

Go to `https://goo.gl/E8DaGb` to access the code.

```
using System;
using System.Collections.Generic;
using System.Text;
namespace RestBuy.Entities
public abstract class BaseEntity
{
    protected int id;
    public int Id => this.id;
}
}
```

4. Have this code inside `Order`:

 Go to `https://goo.gl/7JBmVH` to access the code.

```
using System;
using System.Collections.Generic;
using System.Text;
namespace RestBuy.Entities
{
    public class Order : BaseEntity
    {
        int userId;
        DateTime createDate;
        List<OrderItem> orderItems = new List<OrderItem>();
        private Order() { }
...
...
    }
}
```

5. Have this code inside `OrderItem`:

Go to `https://goo.gl/J11TQu` to access the code.

```
using System;
using System.Collections.Generic;
using System.Text;
namespace RestBuy.Entities
{
  public class OrderItem : BaseEntity
  {
    int productId;
    int quantity;
    decimal price;
    private OrderItem() { }
    public OrderItem(int productId, int quantity, decimal price)
...
...
  }
}
```

6. Have this code inside `Product`:

Go to `https://goo.gl/MPukF3` to access the code.

```
using System;
using System.Collections.Generic;
using System.Text;
namespace RestBuy.Entities
{
  public class Product : BaseEntity
  {
    public string Name { get; set; }
    public string Description { get; set; }
    public decimal Price { get; set; }
    public string PictureUri { get; set; }
    public string Category { get; set; }
  }
}
```

7. Have this code inside `StockAmount`:

 Go to `https://goo.gl/RmgHzn` to access the code.

```
using System;
using System.Collections.Generic;
using System.Text;
namespace RestBuy.Entities
{
    public class StockAmount : BaseEntity
...
...
}
```

Create EF Context and Migrations

For starters, we need to install Entity Framework and its tools to our `Infrastructure` project.

Follow these steps to create the EF context:

1. Just right-click on dependencies and select **Manage NuGet Packages**.
2. Afterwards write `Microsoft.EntityFramework.Core.SqlServer` in the search box and install it.

   Your screen should look as follows:

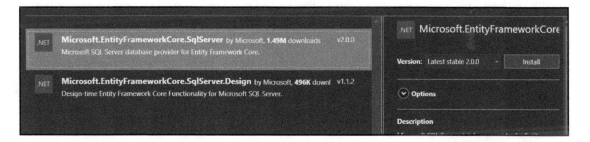

3. Similarly, install the `Microsot.EntityFrameworkCore.Tools` package, as follows:

So, your project folder for `Infrastructure` looks as follows:

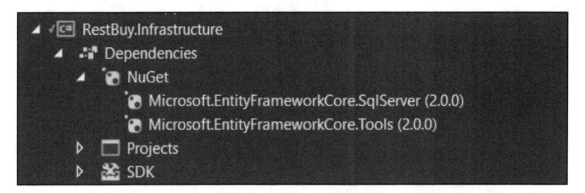

4. Next, we create the `EF` folder in the `Infrastructure` project and implement our `DbContext` with a class called `RestBuyContext`. Make sure you have a reference to the `RestBuy` project from `Infrastructure`. Use this code:

Go to `https://goo.gl/wYLwRA` to access the code.

```
using Microsoft.EntityFrameworkCore;
using Microsoft.EntityFrameworkCore.Metadata.Builders;
using RestBuy.Entities;
using System;
using System.Collections.Generic;
```

```
using System.Text;
...
void ConfigureStockAmount(EntityTypeBuilder<StockAmount> builder)
{
...
  builder.Property(ci =>
ci.Quantity).IsRequired().IsConcurrencyToken();
}
...
```

In the preceding mapping, the Quantity property of StockAmount is marked as ConcurrencyToken as we don't want two orders to reduce the stock amount simultaneously. Suppose that we have two parallel requests racing to buy for the last item. Only one of them can win. Using ConcurrencyToken causes Entity Framework to generate a query that confirms that the value has not been changed. Doing so will cause DbUpdateConcurrencyException; in this case, we have to retry.

Here we use a HiLo algorithm for key generation. If you don't make use of HiLo, normally EF and SQL server uses auto incremented IDs. While auto incremented IDs are simpler, whenever you add an entity to the context, this addition forces the entity to be inserted to the database. That is because we can only retrieve the ID if the actual insertion happens in the case of auto incremented IDs. The HiLo algorithm frees us from this restriction by reserving the IDs beforehand using a database sequence. We also change the defaults for the sequence so that it starts from 1,000 and increments by 100 for each. By using this approach we can insert our design time data to the first 1,000 slots available.

Create migrations

Once we have defined our database context, the next step is to generate migrations. However, since we now have an infrastructure project, we would prefer our infrastructure project to be the host of our migrations.

To do that, follow these steps:

1. Create `RestBuyContextFactory` in the `EF` folder:

 Go to `https://goo.gl/BnBPLD` to access the code.

```
using Microsoft.EntityFrameworkCore;
using Microsoft.EntityFrameworkCore.Design;
using Microsoft.EntityFrameworkCore.Infrastructure;
using RestBuy.Infrastructure.EF;
using System;
using System.Collections.Generic;
using System.Text;
namespace RestBuy.Infrastructure.EF
{
  class RestBuyContextFactory :
IDesignTimeDbContextFactory<RestBuyContext>
  {
    public RestBuyContext CreateDbContext(string[] args)
...
...
  }
}
```

2. Have a look at the folder structure. Our EF folder looks as follows:

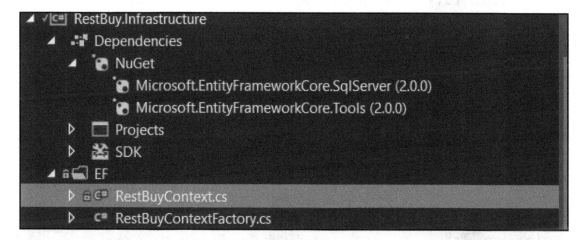

Note that we have our connection string embedded into this factory class. The reason is, as the name of the interface implies, anything that implements `IDesignTimeDbContextFactory` is for design time only. That is, our migration generation tool will make use of this. On the other hand, since we make use of the trusted connection, it is relatively safe to embed it as a string. If it contained any passwords, design time or not, it is a pretty bad idea to embed such strings into the binaries.

3. The obvious next step is to add the migrations. Now let's open package manager, which you can do by typing package into the quick launch search:

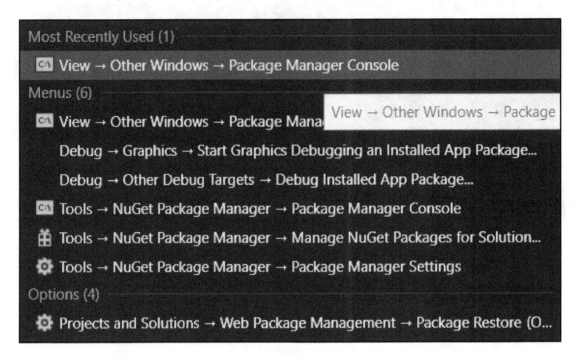

This is what will appear on your screen:

4. Then, make sure you select our Infrastructure project type `Add-MigrationInitialMigration` in the package manager console. Running this command will generate migrations in our `Infrastructure` project:

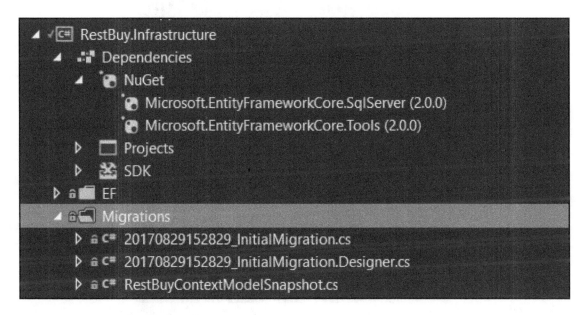

5. Next, we create our database by using the `Update-Database` command:

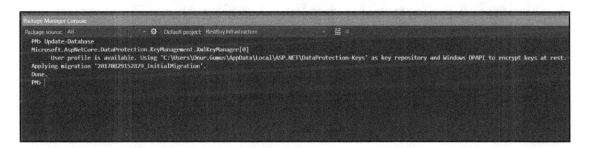

Then, we can see that our tables are created from SQL Server Object Explorer:

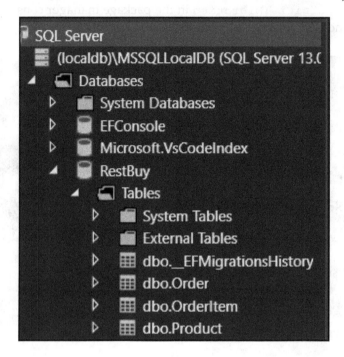

Activity: Adding a Supplier Entity that Denotes the Supplier of a Product

Scenario

You want to add a supplier entity that denotes the supplier of a product.

Aim

Add a supplier entity for a product.

Steps for completion

    1. We can add Supplier class as follows:

Go to `https://goo.gl/pTCc56` to access the code.

```
namespace RestBuy.Entities
{
  class Supplier : BaseEntity
  {
    public string Name { get; set; }
  }
}
```

Optionally we can add a `Supplier` property to `Product` or a `SupplierId` depending on if we want them to be in the same aggregate or not. This is a design choice.

2. And for the migrations we use the following code:

```
void ConfigureSupplier(EntityTypeBuilder<Supplier>builder)
{
  builder.ToTable("Suppliers");
  builder.HasKey(ci => ci.Id);
  builder.Property(ci => ci.Name)
  .IsRequired()
  .HasMaxLength(50);
  builder.HasIndex(c => c.Name).IsUnique();
}
```

Summary

In this chapter, we designed our application. We went on to create the entities for our application. Finally, we looked into creating the EF context and migrations.

8

Adding Features, Testing, and Deployment

In this chapter, we'll look at adding the registration feature to our application. This will be followed by creating a unit test. The objective here is to help you go about with adding a feature and testing it. Finally, we'll upgrade our project to Bootstrap 4.

We will continue implementing our Rest Buy service. This section is relatively critical because we will implement mostly logic to implement our application.

By the end of this chapter, you will be able to:

- Add the registration feature
- Create a unit test
- Upgrade our project to Bootstrap 4
- Deploy Rest Buy to Azure

Adding the Registration Feature

Since we will start adding logic to our application, this is a good time to add our application layer to the project. As we discussed in the previous chapter, we are designing our application to be layered and abiding by domain-driven design standards.

In domain-driven design, a common approach in layering is Onion Architecture. In onion architecture, each layer can make use of the inside layer but the outside layer has to adapt itself to the inside. And we try to design our application from inside out. That's why we have designed our application starting with entities:

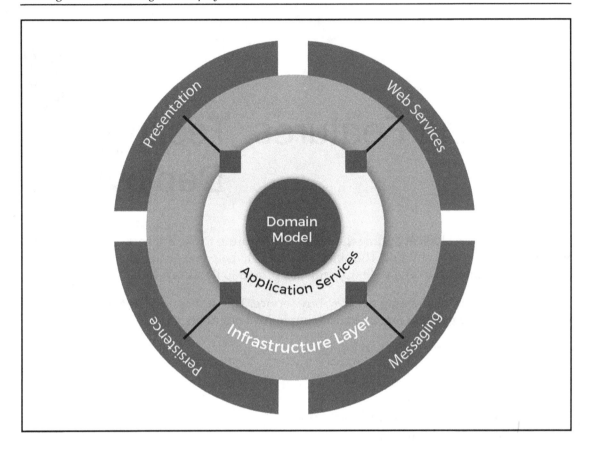

In the preceding figure, we have a domain model at the core, and on top of it we have application services. The purple rectangles are interfaces, the black arrows denote compile-time dependencies, and the magenta circles are external dependencies on infrastructure.

Application Services are for handling commands and requests.

 There is an on-going discussion on whether entities in the domain model should be accessible outside. Some people prefer using DTOs to pass the data evenly between layers. We will not go with that approach here. Instead, we will ensure the entities are immutable from the outside layers.

Sign In and Sign Out Mechanism

For starters, let's begin with our Sign In and Sign Out mechanism. We need a `User` entity for that. So far we haven't created one. Let's create it.

Follow these steps to begin working with our Sign In and Sign Out mechanism:

1. Use the following code:

 Go to `https://goo.gl/cD8tDQ` to access the code.

```
using System;
using System.Collections.Generic;
using System.Linq;
using System.Security.Cryptography;
using System.Text;
namespace RestBuy.Entities
{
  public class User : BaseEntity
  {
...
...
  }
}
```

The interesting thing is that we have defined a hash password algorithm. We also make use of a secret salt. This way, even if our database for passwords is breached, our user passwords will not be easily recovered (of course combined with a strong password policy). By using salt, in this case `secretBytes` and a username, we achieve two things:

- Even if different users have same password, their hashed password values will be different since we include their username.
- We also added a secret keyword directly in the code file, so it will make existing rainbow tables nullified if somebody wants to crack the hash by brute force. We made it a static method because it is more like a utility:

2. Update our `RestBuyContext` by adding the following code:

 Go to `https://goo.gl/wWvhiL` to access the code.

```
void ConfigureUser(EntityTypeBuilder <User> builder)
{
  builder.ToTable(userTable);
  builder.HasKey(ci => ci.Id);
  builder.Property(ci => ci.UserName)
  .IsRequired()
  .HasMaxLength(50);
  builder.Property(ci => ci.Password)
  .IsRequired();
}
```

Our class now looks like this:

 Go to `https://goo.gl/CjSv8g` to access the code.

```
using Microsoft.EntityFrameworkCore;
using Microsoft.EntityFrameworkCore.Metadata.Builders;
using RestBuy.Entities;
using System;
using System.Collections.Generic;
using System.Text;
namespace RestBuy.Infrastructure.EF
{
  public class RestBuyContext : DbContext
  {
...
...
  }
}
```

3. Finally, we add the migration by using `Add-Migration User` in the package manager console:

 Do not forget to change the default project to `Infrastructure`; otherwise, you will get an error.

4. Then we finally update our database:

```
PM> Update-Database
Microsoft.AspNetCore.DataProtection.KeyManagement.XmlKeyManager[0]
User profile is available. Using
'C:\Users\Onur.Gumus\AppData\Local\ASP.NET\DataProtection-Keys' as
key repository and Windows DPAPI to encrypt keys at rest.
Applying migration '20170909141639_User'.
Done.
PM>
```

Creating the Application Layer

For the application layer, we need to create another project.

Follow these steps to start creating the application layer:

1. Create another project, as follows:

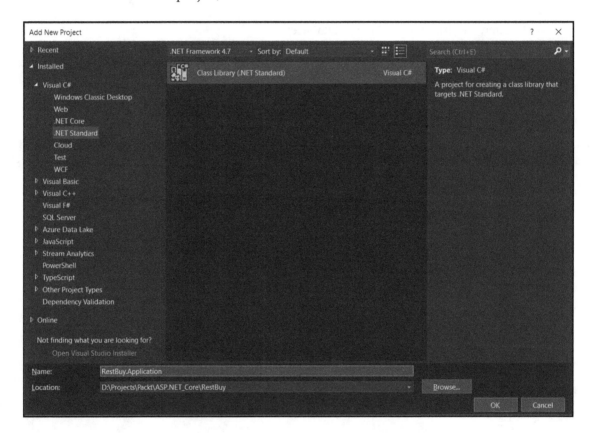

 This project will contain the application service as well as the necessary interfaces required for the external world.

2. We add the reference of `RestBuy` to `RestBuy.Application`, as follows:

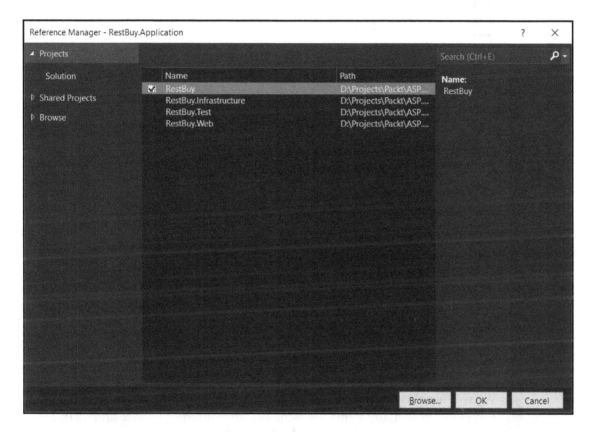

3. Next, we will start to define our interfaces. For starters, let's define an `IQuery<T>` interface in `Services/Queries` (create these folders if they don't exist) folder in the `RestBuy.Application` project as follows:

 Go to `https://goo.gl/K9QpWN` to access the code.

```
using RestBuy.Entities;
using System;
using System.Linq.Expressions;
namespace RestBuy.Application.Services.Queries
{
    public interface IQuery<T> where T : BaseEntity
    {
```

```
        Expression<Func<T, bool>> Criteria { get; }
        int Take { get; }
...
...
      int Skip { get; }
      }
    }
```

4. Add a default implementation in `BaseQuery`, as shown:

Go to `https://goo.gl/HNHd9k` to access the code.

```
using RestBuy.Entities;
using System;
using System.Collections.Generic;
using System.Linq.Expressions;
using System.Text;
namespace RestBuy.Application.Services.Queries
{
    public abstract class BaseQuery<T> : IQuery<T> where T:
BaseEntity
...
...
}
```

We will use this interface to query our repositories. The `Take` property represents how many items we want to take from the database and `Skip` is used for setting how many items to skip. These properties are used for the paging of the records. We will also define a lambda expression that denotes the filtering.

5. Next, define the base repo for all entities in the `Repos` folder (again create it if it doesn't exist) of the `RestBuy.Application` project:

 Go to `https://goo.gl/nzouBU` to access the code.

```
using RestBuy.Entities;
using System;
using System.Collections.Generic;
using System.Text;
using System.Threading;
using System.Threading.Tasks;
using RestBuy.Application.Services.Queries;
namespace RestBuy.Application.Repos
{
   public interface IEntityRepo<T> where T : BaseEntity
   {
      Task<T> GetById(int id, CancellationToken cancellationToken =
default);
      Task<List<T>> ListAsync(IQuery<T> query = null,
CancellationToken cancellationToken = default);
   }
}
```

 When using default keyword, the IDE will warn you if you want to use the latest version of C#. Comply to it.

We are using `Task` because most database operations are asynchronous and cancellable (indeed, most IO operations are).

6. Then, we define our `IUserRepo` interface as follows:

 Go to `https://goo.gl/Uykbex` to access the code.

```
using RestBuy.Entities;
using System.Threading;
using System.Threading.Tasks;
namespace RestBuy.Application.Repos
{
```

```
public interface IUserRepo : IEntityRepo<User>
{
    Task AddAsync(User user, CancellationToken ct = default());
}
}
```

We have only defined an `Add` method here, because for the time being we only plan to add users. Depending on our needs, we can then modify this interface.

7. Finally, we define an IUoW interface, which stands for Unit of Work, as follows:

 Go to `https://goo.gl/ePL5Fc` to access the code.

```
using System.Threading;
using System.Threading.Tasks;
namespace RestBuy.Application.Repos
{
    public interface IUoW
    {
        Task SaveChangesAsync(CancellationToken cancellationToken =
default);
    }
}
```

 UoW represents a database transaction.

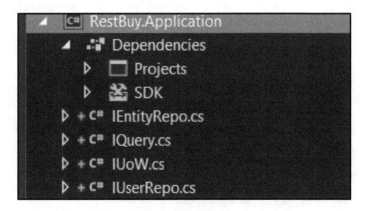

Next, let's do the implementations in the Infrastructure project.

Performing Implementations in the Infrastructure Project

Follow these steps to perform implementations in the `Infrastructure` project:

1. We first add a reference to our `Application` project from `Infrastructure`:

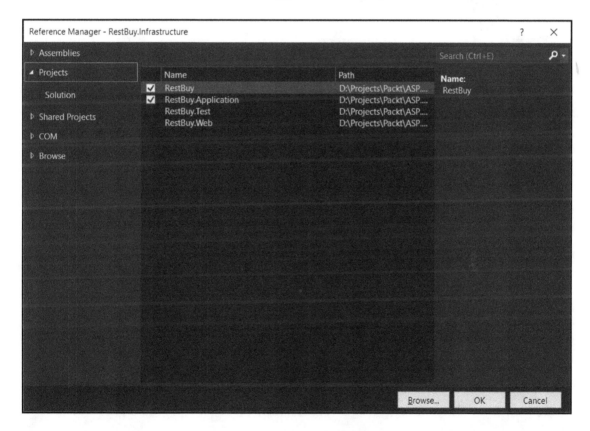

2. Then we implement our interfaces, starting with IUoW in the `EF` folder of the `Infrastructure` project:

Go to `https://goo.gl/SFBMLt` to access the code.

```
using RestBuy.Application.Repos;
using System.Threading;
using System.Threading.Tasks;
namespace RestBuy.Infrastructure.EF
{
  public class RestBuyUoW : IUoW
  {
...
...
  }
}
```

3. Next, define a `BaseRepo` that will be the base class for all our repository implementations:

 Go to `https://goo.gl/s7LVBU` to access the code.

```
using Microsoft.EntityFrameworkCore;
using RestBuy.Application.Repos;
using RestBuy.Application.Services.Queries;
using RestBuy.Entities;
using System.Collections.Generic;
using System.Linq;
using System.Threading;
using System.Threading.Tasks;
namespace RestBuy.Infrastructure.EF
{
...
  if (query.Skip > 0)
  {
    filterQuery = filterQuery.Skip(query.Skip);
  }
  if (query.Take > 0)
  {
    filterQuery = filterQuery.Take(query.Take);
  }
  if (query.OrderBy != null || query.OrderByDescending != null)
...
}
```

The preceding code basically checks if the query has to do with either `Take`, `Skip`, or `OrderBy` clauses, and modifies the query accordingly (depending on these parts of queries defined).

4. Now, define the `UserRepo`:

Go to `https://goo.gl/9wPekN` to access the code.

```
using RestBuy.Application.Repos;
using RestBuy.Entities;
using System.Threading;
using System.Threading.Tasks;
namespace RestBuy.Infrastructure.EF
{
  public class UserRepo : BaseRepo<User> , IUserRepo
  {
    public UserRepo(RestBuyContext restBuyContext) :
base(restBuyContext)
    { }
    public Task AddAsync(User user, CancellationToken ct = default)
=>
    this.restBuyContext.Users.AddAsync(user, ct);
  }
}
```

Our EF folder looks as follows:

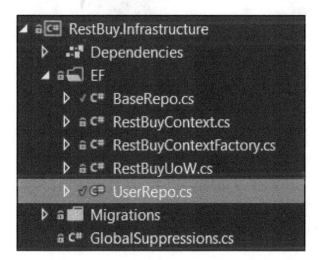

Finally, we need to define our service interfaces. We will start with user registration. For starters, let's define our ViewModel for registration. We will define the ViewModel directly in the application layer as this will be the input of our service interfaces. Normally in onion layered architecture, we try not to pass data across the layer borders. That's why we are not directly using the entities. One notable exception to this rule is persistence. Since the persistence layer is responsible only for persisting entities, there is no harm passing the entities directly there. Still, this is a hotly debated subject.

Defining our ViewModel for Registration

Follow these steps to define our ViewModel for registration:

1. Let's create a `ViewModels` folder in the `RestBuy.Application` project and add a class called `NewUserViewModel`:

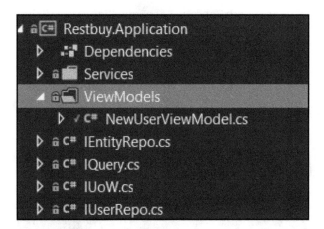

2. Use this code inside `NewUserViewModel`:

 Go to `https://goo.gl/ATiDPz` to access the code.

```
using RestBuy.Entities;
using System.ComponentModel.DataAnnotations;
namespace RestBuy.Application.ViewModels
{
    public class NewUserViewModel
    {
```

```
[Required, MaxLength(50)]
public string Username { get; set; }
[Required, DataType(DataType.Password)]
public string Password { get; set; }
[DataType(DataType.Password), Compare
(nameof(Password))]
public string ConfirmPassword { get; set; }
  internal User CreateUser() =>
new User(this.Username, this.Password);
  }
}
```

 Make sure you add `System.ComponentModel.DataAnnotations.dll` from the Assemblies Framework section of the Add References popup.

Note the `CreateUser` model. This method builds a `User` object from the `ViewModel`. Alternatively, we could have used a factory pattern. Note that we marked the method internal. That is for when we don't want these kinds of factory methods called from other layers.

3. Create the `Services` folder to host our services and define `IRegistrationService`:

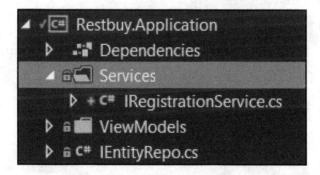

4. Have this code inside `IRegistrationService`:

 Go to `https://goo.gl/wNEq3F` to access the code.

```
using RestBuy.Application.ViewModels;
using System.Threading;
```

```
using System.Threading.Tasks;
namespace RestBuy.Application.Services
{
   public interface IRegistrationService
   {
      Task RegisterUser(NewUserViewModel newUserViewModel,
CancellationToken token = default);
   }
}
```

5. Next, add the reference of our application project to the web project:

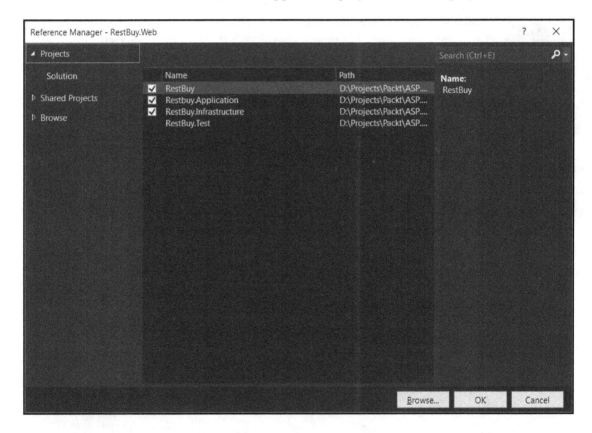

Finally, we can start defining our controllers. For starters, let's define our `Accounts` controller. You can delete the existing `HomeController`.

Defining our Controllers

Follow these steps to define our controllers:

1. Create a new controller in the `Controllers` folder by right-clicking on the `Controllers` folder, adding a new item, and then selecting the MVC controller class:

And our Web project looks as follows:

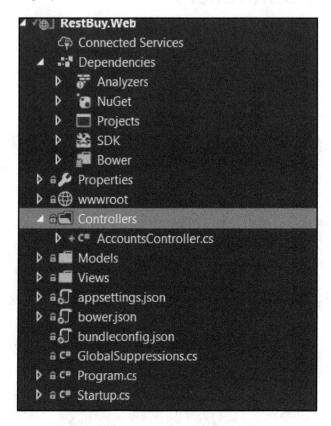

2. As for RESTful practices, when a GET request comes to our Accounts controller, we will return a registration form. Use this code:

```csharp
using Microsoft.AspNetCore.Mvc;
namespace RestBuy.Web.Controllers
{
  [Route("[controller]")]
  public class AccountsController : Controller
  {
    [HttpGet]
    public IActionResult RegistrationForm()
    {
    return View();
    }
  }
}
```

3. Define our view:

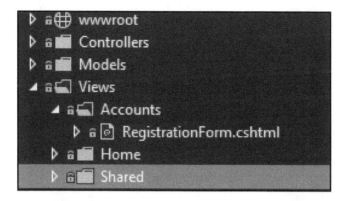

4. Add the following code into it:

Go to `https://goo.gl/SvE6Qv` to access the code.

```
@model RestBuy.Application.ViewModels.NewUserViewModel
@{
 ViewBag.Title = "Register";
}
<h1>Register</h1>
<form method="post" >
 <div asp-validation-summary="ModelOnly"></div>
 ...
 ...
 <div>
 <input type="submit" value="Register" />
 </div>
</form>
```

We have not specified any path for posting in our form, because we will post to the same URL as with this page.

Now if we run our application and try to visit our AccXounts page from `http://localhost:49163/Accounts` (your port number might be different), we will end up with the following form:

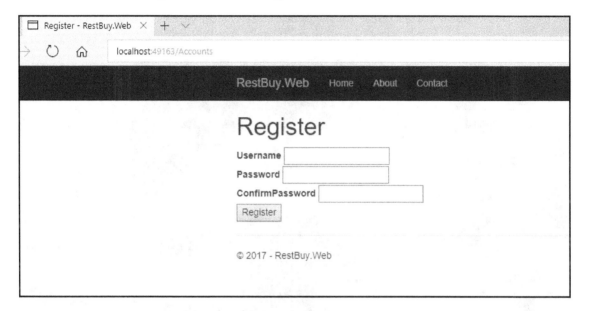

Obviously, the form doesn't look aligned but that's something we will fix later.

We also need a landing page when the registration is successful.

Creating the Post-Registration Landing Page

Follow these steps to create the post-registration landing page:

1. We could use the same form page, but in this case, we will create
   `SuccesfullyRegistered.cshtml` in the `Accounts` folder, as follows:

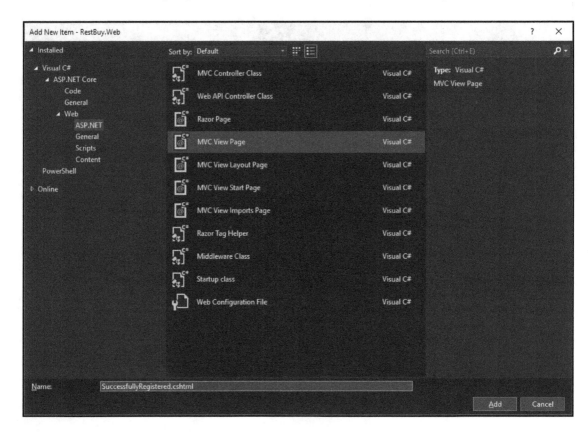

2. Use the following code:

```
@{
    ViewBag.Title = "Registration Successful";
}
<h1>You have registered successfully!</h1>
<ul>
  <li><a asp-action="" asp-controller="">Home</a></li>
  <li><a asp-action="" asp-controller="">Login</a></li>
</ul>
```

3. In the preceding code, we will fill in the necessary action and controller fields later. Although this page is simplistic, for the purpose of this demo, it is acceptable for the time being. The final step is to revise our controller, as follows:

```
using Microsoft.AspNetCore.Mvc;
using RestBuy.Application.Services;
using RestBuy.Application.ViewModels;
using System.Threading;
using System.Threading.Tasks;
namespace RestBuy.Web.Controllers
{
    [Route("[controller]")]
...
...
}
```

We have added our `IRegistrationService` to the constructor. Our service will simply be injected by ASP.NET runtime once we have registered it against a concrete service, which we haven't written yet.

Secondly, we have defined a `Register` method that gets the ViewModel and a cancellation token. The cancellation token is entirely optional here. ASP.NET runtime has a smart behavior: whenever the HTTP request is aborted from the client side, it will trigger the cancellation token. Generally, it is recommended to pass the cancellation tokens for any I/O call. In this case, we will query the database, but feel free to skip it if you find this approach too verbose. Next, we will check whether our ViewModel is valid or not.

 Remember that we have decorated our view model with few attributes. At the model binding phase, ASP.NET Runtime automatically validates our model and sets the model state accordingly. If our model is valid, then we proceed with the registration by calling the registration service and returning the view.

If our view is not valid, we will show the very same form page along with its validation errors, which are automatically displayed.

At this point, we recommend you write a unit test against the controller to verify the behavior, but we will skip that and directly implement our registration service. Our registration service has to check whether such a user exists in the database. So, let's first create a query for it, which will get implemented from `IQuery<User>`.

Creating a Query for the Registration Service

We create query objects instead of using linq because these kinds of queries are associated with the business logic, and wrapping queries into objects allows us to reuse them as well as unit test them. Also, naming them with a class gives us more clues about the purpose of the query rather than on-the-fly queries.

Follow these steps to create a query for the registration service:

In the Queries folder of the Application project, we create a UserExistsQuery class, as follows:

 Go to https://goo.gl/3r92QU to access the code.

```
using RestBuy.Entities;
using System;
using System.Linq.Expressions;
namespace RestBuy.Application.Services.Queries
{
  class UserExistsQuery : BaseQuery<User>
  {
    public UserExistsQuery(string userName) =>
      this.UserName = userName;
    public string UserName { get; }
    public override Expression<Func<User, bool>>
    Criteria =>
      u => u.UserName == this.UserName;
    public override int Take => 1;
  }
}
```

Basically, this query object searches for a user with a given username, and attempts to take the first record by setting Take = 1.

 Remember, one of the goals of software engineering is to have readable and understandable code. Short code doesn't always mean good code. So whenever necessary, feel free to create new classes and name them properly.

Validating the Registration

Follow these steps to validate the registration:

1. We do our service implementations in `Services/Core` folder. Our service implementation is as follows:

Go to `https://goo.gl/Xxv3kj` to access the code.

```
using RestBuy.Application.ViewModels;
using RestBuy.Application.Repos;
using RestBuy.Application.Services.Queries;
using System.ComponentModel.DataAnnotations;
using System.Threading;
using System.Threading.Tasks;
using RestBuy.Application.Services;
namespace Restbuy.Application.Services.Core
{
  public class RestBuyRegistrationService : IRegistrationService
  {
    readonly IUserRepo userRepo;
    readonly IUoW uow;
...
...
  }
}
```

At the constructor, our Unit of Work is injected. Then we fulfil our interface contract. By using validation context, we validate our view model once more. Although we will validate the view model in the controller, the application is not (and should not be) aware.

As a security practice, inner layers should not trust upper layers when it comes to data validation.

2. Since we are throwing a validation exception from our application layer, our controller should handle and show a validation message with respect to that. We revise our register method as follows:

 Go to `https://goo.gl/KWuyPd` to access the code.

```
[HttpPost]
public async Task<IActionResult> Register(NewUserViewModel
newUserViewModel, CancellationToken cancellationToken)
{
    if (ModelState.IsValid)
    {
...
...
    }
    return View(nameof(RegistrationForm));
}
```

 Don't forget to add `using System.ComponentModel.DataAnnotations;` at the beginning of the file.

In case a validation error occurs, we will show it in the registration page.

3. Then, we invoke our user exists query and get the users with the same name. If a username already exists, our `userList` will have a count greater than 0 (it will be actually 1 since we know our query makes use of Take = 1). In that case, we need to reject the registration. Otherwise we register the user by getting `UserRepo` from the UoW, add it to the user repo, and commit the changes by calling `SaveChangesAsync`.

 There may be trouble if two requests come with the same username registration request. Although this is a tiny possibility, a malicious user can try to break our data.

Our current code doesn't check these parallel requests and doesn't have to. For these kind of requests, we should put a unique constraint in the database. Database constraints are your last line of defense. Because the odds are tiny for such a thing to happen (except for the malicious user case), your unique constraint will fail and you will show an error page telling the user a problem occurred and they should retry the operation. So our next step will be to add our unique index to the `Username` property.

4. Add the unique index to the `UserName` property by modifying the `ConfigureUser` method of the `RestBuyContext`, as follows:

Go to `https://goo.gl/Ncc42w` to access the code.

```
void ConfigureUser(EntityTypeBuilder<User> builder)
{
  builder.ToTable(userTable);
  builder.HasKey(ci => ci.Id);
  builder.Property(ci => ci.UserName)
    .IsRequired()
    .HasMaxLength(50);
  builder.HasIndex(c => c.UserName).IsUnique();
  builder.Property(ci => ci.Password)
    .IsRequired();
}
```

Note that we have added the `HasIndex` method.

5. Now, we need to upgrade our migrations and database by executing the following commands in the package manager console:

```
Add-Migration AddUsernameIndex
Update-Database
```

Make sure you select `RestBuy.Infrastructure` before running the commands from the default project combobox.

Our application project now looks as follows:

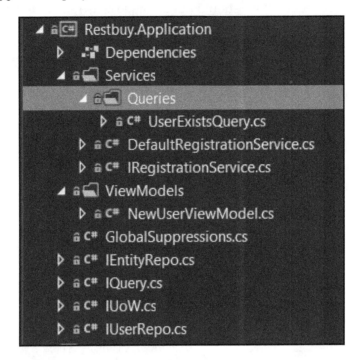

6. Lastly, we need to create our service registrations. Since we have used interfaces and their implementations, we will associate these interfaces with their implementations with the built-in dependency injection mechanism. In the web project, we will update the `ConfigureServices` method in `Startup.cs`, as follows:

 Go to `https://goo.gl/NJ2zvC` to access the code.

```
public void ConfigureServices(IServiceCollection services)
{
    services.AddEntityFrameworkSqlServer()
    .AddDbContext<RestBuyContext>(options =>
    options.UseSqlServer(Configuration.
    GetConnectionString("DefaultConnection")));
    services.AddScoped<IRegistrationService,
    RestBuyRegistrationService>();
    services.AddScoped<IUoW, RestBuyUoW>();
```

```
services.AddScoped<IUserRepo, UserRepo>();
services.AddMvc();
}
```

So, we make three registrations: IRegistrationService to
DefaultRegistrationService, IUoW to RestBuyUoW, and IUserRepo to
UserRepo. We used the scope approach so that only one instance of these services
is created per request. And they will be disposed of at the end of each request.

7. Next let's set up our connection string. We edit appsettings.json in the Web
   project:

 Go to https://goo.gl/zTgTcc to access the code.

```
{
  "ConnectionStrings":
  {
    "DefaultConnection": "Server=(localdb)\\
    mssqllocaldb;Database=RestBuy;Trusted_
    Connection=True;MultipleActiveResultSets=true"
  },
  "Logging":
  {
    "IncludeScopes": false,
    "LogLevel":
    {
      "Default": "Warning"
    }
  }
}
```

Now we can run our application. We should visit the /Accounts page to see the registration form:

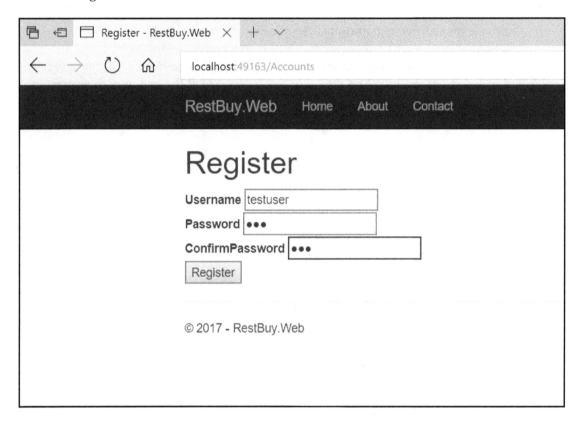

After the registration is successful, we are redirected to the Registration Successful page:

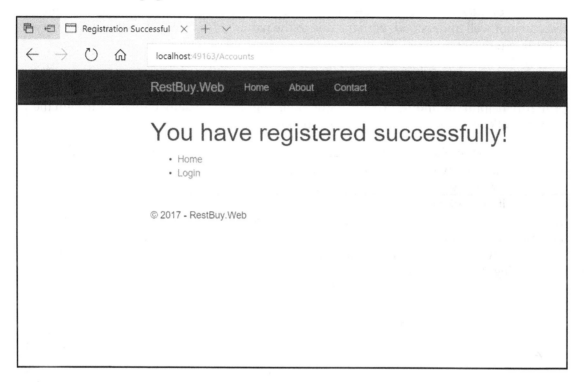

And if we check our database, we can see our user has been inserted, as shown here:

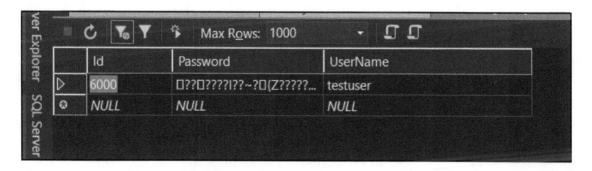

Creating a Unit Test

In the last decade unit tests have become popular. But many times, the true goal of unit tests are not well understood, perhaps due to the naming. It's true that unit tests are very helpful in terms of finding bugs in our software.

It is useful to write unit test even if you have a function with a small amount of code. The reason is although unit tests are for hunting bugs there is one category of bugs they are primarily helpful for finding. That is regression. Regression usually happens through the breakage of existing functionality as we add new code.

With regard to regression, a unit tests acts like a fusebox. It will ensure that if we break existing functionality without realising, the older tests start to fail. And if they don't, the programmer will feel comfortable as he or she would know that it is unlikely that existing functionality is broken. Although unit tests do not guarantee this kind of safety, it is an invaluable asset if you constantly add to or change your code. Many people treat unit tests as a specification of the application written in code. There's no denying that test-driven development has recently evolved into behavior-driven development, where developers start writing the formal specs of the application as a unit test.

Writing a Unit Test

Follow these steps to write a unit test for our application:

1. Let's create a unit test. Let's name it `RestBuy.Test`, as shown in the following screenshot:

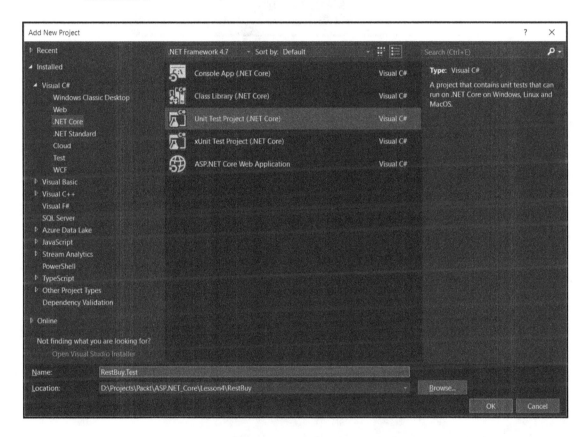

2. Rename `UnitTest1.cs` to `EFTest` and copy `appsettings.json` from your web project to the test project. But change the database name to `RestBuy_Test`.

 Make sure you add references to all other projects from Test. You also need a reference to `Microsoft.EntityFramework.Core`, and then install `Microsoft.Extensions.Configuration` from NuGet.

Your project should look as shown here:

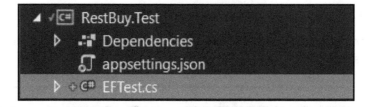

3. Now, ensure your `appsettings.json` file resembles this:

```
{
    "ConnectionStrings":
    {
        "DefaultConnection": "Server=(localdb)\\mssqllocaldb;
        Database=RestBuy_Test;Trusted_Connection=True;
        MultipleActiveResultSets=true"
    },
    "Logging":
    {
        "IncludeScopes": false,
        "LogLevel":
        {
            "Default": "Warning"
        }
    }
}
```

4. Right-click on the `appsettings.json` file from **Properties** ensure it is deployed to the output folder by selecting **Copy if newer** for the **Copy to Output Directory** option:

5. Ensure your `EFTest` file also resembles this:

 Go to `https://goo.gl/NK99He` to access the code.

```
using Microsoft.EntityFrameworkCore;
using Microsoft.Extensions.Configuration;
using Microsoft.VisualStudio.TestTools.UnitTesting;
using RestBuy.Entities;
using RestBuy.Infrastructure.EF;
using System.IO;
using System.Threading.Tasks;
```

```
namespace RestBuy.Test
{
...
...
}
```

This test basically creates our database, saves a product to the database in one context, then queries it in another context and commits it.

Running the Unit Test

Follow these steps to run the unit test:

1. Now, to run the test, build the solution first and open Test Explorer from the **Test** menu as shown here:

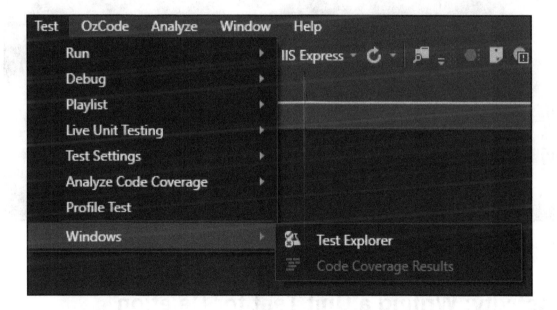

2. Then right-click on the test and run it:

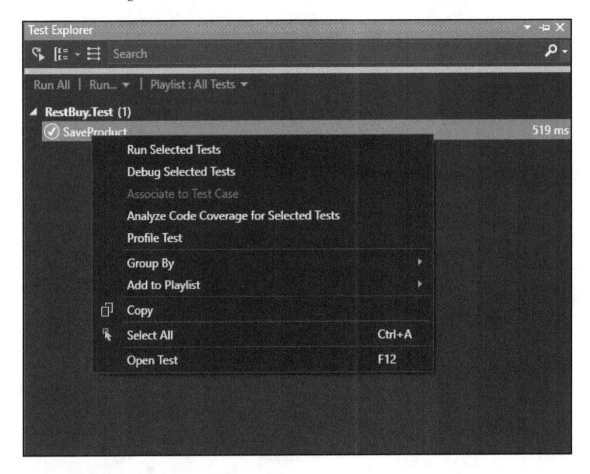

This concludes our basic model creation.

Activity: Writing a Unit Test for Deletion

Scenario

Write a unit test that tests deletion of a product.

Steps for completion

1. We can refactor our test as follows:

 Go to `https://goo.gl/EUCb5B` to access the code.

```
using Microsoft.EntityFrameworkCore;
using Microsoft.Extensions.Configuration;
using Microsoft.VisualStudio.TestTools.UnitTesting;
using RestBuy.Entities;
using RestBuy.Infrastructure.EF;
using System.IO;
using System.Threading.Tasks;
namespace RestBuy.Test
{
  [TestClass]
  public class EFTest
  {
...
...
  }
}
```

2. Now to run the test, build the solution first and open Test Explorer from the **Test** menu as shown here:

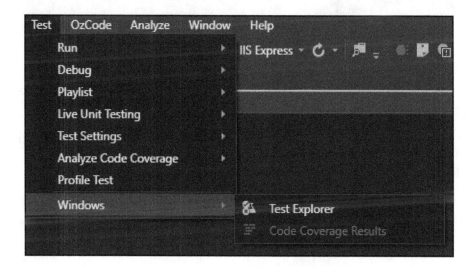

3. Then right-click on the test and run it:

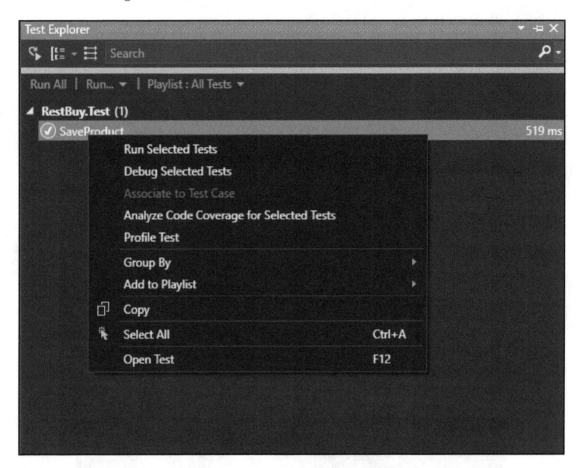

Upgrading Our Project to Bootstrap 4

In newer versions of Visual Studio, Bower has been removed. We'll look at upgrading our project to Bootstrap manually. If you are using ASP.NET Core 2.2 or newer, you may not have to do the following steps as these newer versions come with Bootstrap 4.

Follow these steps to our project to Bootstrap:

1. Open `_Layout.cshtml`. Update your script references, as follows:

 Go to `https://goo.gl/GtuEk7` to access the code.

```
<!DOCTYPE html>
<html>
<head>
...
<link rel="stylesheet"
href="https://maxcdn.bootstrapcdn.com/bootstrap/4.0.0-beta.3/css/bo
otstrap.min.css" integrity="sha384-
Zug+QiDoJOrZ5t4lssLdxGhVrurbmBWopoEl+
M6BdEfwnCJZtKxi1KgxUyJq13dy" crossorigin="anonymous">
...
</body>
</html>
```

Note that we should add popper as a UMD module and before bootstrap in the script sections. Also, we added the `ValidationScriptsPartial` page. That file is generated by the Visual Studio template and includes the client-side validation code that is necessary.

2. Inside the `ValidationScriptsPartial.cshtml` file, we make the following changes so that it adds relevant Bootstrap styles in case of failures:

 Go to `https://goo.gl/xud8jd` to access the code.

```
<environment include="Development">
  <script src="~/lib/jquery-
validation/dist/jquery.validate.js"></script>
  <script src="~/lib/jquery-validation-
unobtrusive/jquery.validate.unobtrusive.js"></script>
</environment>
...
...
</script>
```

3. Next, we revise the registration form with Bootstrap:

 Go to `https://goo.gl/ad7JYA` to access the code.

```
@model Restbuy.Application.ViewModels.NewUserViewModel
@{
ViewBag.Title = "Register";
}
<h1>Register</h1>
<form method="post">
  <div asp-validation-summary="ModelOnly"></div>
  <div class="form-group">
...
...
</form>
```

This is what will show up on your screen:

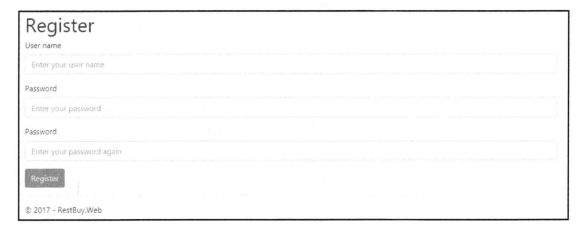

Our form now looks much better in the `/Accounts` URL.

4. Now let's click on the **Register** button.

That looks good, but our password field looks green, as if it is valid. The reason it is green is that we forgot to add the `Required` property to our `ViewModel` the `ConfirmPassword` field.

5. Update `NewUserViewModel`:

Go to `https://goo.gl/7YN6ke` to access the code.

```
using RestBuy.Entities;
using System.ComponentModel.DataAnnotations;
namespace RestBuy.Application.ViewModels
{
  public class NewUserViewModel
  {
    [Required, MaxLength(50)]
...
...
  }
}
```

6. After that, run our page again:

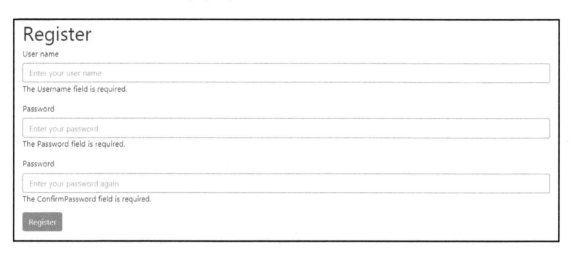

This time we successfully see three red boxes. Note that even if we disable the JavaScript validation, our form is still guarded from the server side. It's just that in this case we won't see these red lines as they are generated by JavaScript. Also note that errors occurring if the same user exists cannot be easily covered by client-side validation. Instead, we will utilize `ValidationTagHelper`.

7. Add a `TagHelpers` folder to your Web project and create the `ValidationClassTagHelper` class, as follows:

 Go to `https://goo.gl/3CBcBe` to access the code.

```
using Microsoft.AspNetCore.Mvc.Rendering;
using Microsoft.AspNetCore.Mvc.TagHelpers;
using Microsoft.AspNetCore.Mvc.ViewFeatures;
using Microsoft.AspNetCore.Razor.TagHelpers;
using System.Linq;
namespace RestBuy.Web.TagHelpers
{
...
...
}
```

The preceding class simply sets the appropriate Bootstrap class depending on the value's validity.

8. Change your `ViewImports.chtml` file in the `Views` folder as follows:

```
@using RestBuy.Web
@using RestBuy.Web.Models
@addTagHelper *, Microsoft.AspNetCore.Mvc.TagHelpers
@addTagHelper *, RestBuy.Web
```

9. Change `RegistrationForm.cshtml`, as follows:

 Go to `https://goo.gl/TGhPzF` to access the code.

```
@model RestBuy.Application.ViewModels.NewUserViewModel
@{
    ViewBag.Title = "Register";
}
<h1>Register</h1>
...
...
</form>
```

Note that we added the `bootrap-validation` attribute to the input fields.

10. All is well; now, we have to cover on caveat. The password fields will be emptied on an invalid post by the ASP.NET runtime. But if we leave them as it is, they will also appear green despite the fact they are empty. So we want to mark those password field validation steps as skipped if they are valid. This is so that they will never look green and empty. To do this, we change our controller method as follows:

 Go to `https://goo.gl/PpWxDY` to access the code.

```
[HttpPost]
public async Task<IActionResult> Register(
NewUserViewModel newUserViewModel,
CancellationToken cancellationToken)
{
    if (ModelState.IsValid)
```

```
    {
    try
...
...
    }
    return View(nameof(RegistrationForm));
}
```

 Make sure you add using `Microsoft.AspNetCore.Mvc.ModelBinding;` at the top of the file.

11. Now, if we try to register with an existing user, we get this:

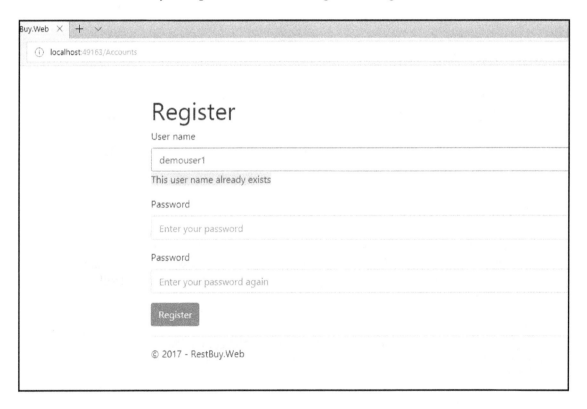

12. Finally, we utilize Bootstrap for the successful registration in the `SuccessfullyRegistered` page, by using this code:

Go to `https://goo.gl/C9F1nz` to access the code.

```
@{
    ViewBag.Title = "Registration Successful";
}
<div class="alert alert-success" role="alert">
    <h4 class="alertheading">You have registered successfully!!</h4>
</div>
<ul class="nav">
    <li class="nav-item">
        <a class="nav-link" asp-action="" asp-controller="">Home</a>
    </li>
    <li class="nav-item">
        <a class="nav-link" asp-action="" asp-controller="">Login</a>
    </li>
</ul>
```

Now, our `SuccessfullyRegistered` page manifests itself as follows:

You have registered successfully!!

Home   Login

© 2017 - RestBuy.Web

We should write unit tests to prevent regression. As of now, Bower has been deprecated and using NPM is recommended.
We can style our application and even style the validation. We can style our application and even style the validation using Bootstrap.

Activity: Adding a EULA Agreement

Scenario

You want to add an end user license agreement (EULA) to prevent user to register without checking it.

Aim

Add an end-user license agreement to the application

Steps for completion

1. Modify `NewUserViewModel`, as follows:

 Go to `https://goo.gl/nKcvUq` to access the code.

```
using RestBuy.Entities;
using System.ComponentModel.DataAnnotations;
namespace RestBuy.Application.ViewModels
{
...
  public bool TermsAndConditions { get; set; }
  internal User CreateUser() =>
    new User(this.Username, this.Password);
  }
}
```

Note that we have added a `TermsAndConditions` validator with a range validator that can only be true.

2. Then modify the registration page as follows:

 Go to `https://goo.gl/uUxNau` to access the code.

```
@model RestBuy.Application.ViewModels.NewUserViewModel
@{
  ViewBag.Title = "Register";
}
<h1>Register</h1>
...
...
    <input class="btn btn-primary" type="submit" value="Register"
/>
  </div>
</form>
```

3. To the bottom of the _ValidationScriptsPartial file, add the following:

 Go to https://goo.gl/P6GBey to access the code.

```
<script>
// extend jquery range validator to work for required checkboxes
var defaultRangeValidator = $.validator.methods.range;
$.validator.methods.range = function (value, element, param)
{
  if (element.type === 'checkbox')
  {
    // if it's a checkbox return true if it is checked
    return element.checked;
  }
  else
  {
    // otherwise run the default validation function
    return defaultRangeValidator.call(this, value, element, param);
  }
}
</script>
```

Now our form looks as follows:

Deploying RestBuy to Azure

Microsoft Azure is a cloud computing platform and infrastructure from Microsoft for building, deploying, and managing applications and services. It supports different programming languages and arrays of services.

You can deploy your application in any server with **Internet Information Service** (**IIS**) in your network. But this restricts your application to being accessed only from within your network, assuming your server could only be accessed from within your network (as in most network setups). In this section, we are going to deploy the ASP.NET Core application in Microsoft Azure so that your users across the globe can access your application.

Signing up to Microsoft Azure

In order for your application to be deployed to Azure, you need to have an account with Azure. You can create an Azure account for free and you'll have sufficient credits to deploy your application for free within the first 30 days (`https://azure.microsoft.com/`).

To sign up perform the following steps:

1. Go to `https://azure.microsoft.com/. You'll see this page on your screen:`
2. Click on the **Start free** button or FREE ACCOUNT link (at the top right-hand corner of the page):
3. You'll be redirected to the following page. Enter your Microsoft account credentials and click on the **Sign In** button. If you don't have a Microsoft account, you can create one by clicking on the **Sign Up** now link at the bottom of the page:

> These pages may appear differently than what's shown in the screenshots because of regular Microsoft updates, but the actions you should take are the same.

4. Once you have signed-in, you will be asked for details about your country, first name, second name, and your work phone, as follows:
5. Once you have entered all the necessary details, you will be asked for your country code and phone number so that Azure can text you or call you to verify you are a real person and not a robot. If you choose the option of text me, you will get a code to your mobile phone; you need to enter it in the last field and click on **Verify Code**.
6. Once you have been verified by phone, you need to enter your credit card information in the following form. You'll be billed for approximately $1 and it will be refunded within five to six business days back to your account. This information is collected to identify the user's identity and the user will not be billed unless the user explicitly opted for the paid service.

7. Once you enter your credit card information and click on **Next**, you will have to agree to the subscription agreement as the final step in the sign-up process.

8. Once the sign-up process completes, you'll be shown the following screen. You'll also get a confirmation e-mail (to the e-mail ID that you gave in the first step) with the subscription details:

Prerequisites to Azure Deployment

In order to publish the ASP.NET Core application to Azure from the Visual Studio 2017 Community Edition, perform the following steps:

1. Start **Visual Studio Installer** as shown here:
2. And then your selections should look like the following:
3. Then you click on the **Modify** button at the bottom right and your download starts.

Now let's publish Rest Buy to Azure. One thing we should be careful is that we have database migrations to run. Normally by default if we had our migrations defined in the web project, then the wizard automatically asks if we want to generate the migrations as well. However, we have defined our migrations within the Infrastructure project. In this case we have to add some code so that whenever our application accesses RestBuyContext it will generate the migrations if there is any.

Deploying Rest Buy to Azure

Follow these steps to deploy Rest Buy to Azure:

1. Alter our RestBuyContext, as follows:

```
public class RestBuyContext : DbContext
{
  const string hiloName = "order_hilo";
  const string productTable = "Product";
  const string orderTable = "Order";
  const string orderItemTable = "OrderItem";
  const string userTable = "User";
  static bool initialized;
...
...
}
/// rest of the code remains the same
```

Basically in the code, we added a static initialized property that is called only the very first time when our constructor is invoked. We don't want to check if migrations are applied each time we create our context; rather we want it once per application start. The `Database.Migrate()` method ensures that necessary migrations are applied. Once we have defined this, we can proceed with our publishing as usual.

2. Right-click on the `Web` project from the solution explorer and select **Publish**. You will get the following screen:
3. From `Services`, create a new database for our application as shown in the following screenshot by clicking on the plus sign and filling the necessary form items, as shown:
4. After filling the preceding form and clicking on **Create**, click on **Settings** in the **Publish** pane. Select the **DefaultConnection** checkbox, (Note that it may take few seconds for this checkbox to appear.) as shown:
5. Click on **Save** and then click on **Publish**. Doing so will publish our application and run it. This is the screen for registration:
6. Clicking on **Register** will yield this:

Summary

We've looked into implementing the registration feature. We created a unit test for it. We upgraded our project to Bootstrap 4. Finally, we deployed our application to Microsoft Azure. Well done! We've completed this course successfully.

Other Books You May Enjoy

If you enjoyed this book, you may be interested in these other books by Packt:

Learning ASP.NET Core 2.0
ASP.NET Core 2 and Vue.js

ISBN: 9781-78883-946-4

- Setup a modern development environment for building both client-side and server-side code
- Use Vue CLI to scaffold front-end applications
- Build and compose a set of Vue.js components
- Setup and configure client-side routing to introduce multiple pages into a SPA
- Integrate popular CSS frameworks with Vue.js to build a product catalogue
- Build a functioning shopping cart that persists its contents across browser sessions
- Build client-side forms with immediate validation feedback using an open-source library dedicated to Vue.js form validation
- Refactor backend application to use the OpenIddict library

Mastering ASP.NET Core 2.0
Ricardo Peres

ISBN: 978-1-78728-3688

- Get to know the new features of ASP.NET Core 2.0
- Find out how to configure ASP.NET Core
- Configure routes to access ASP.NET Core resources
- Create controllers and action methods and see how to maintain the state
- Create views to display contents
- Implement and validate forms and retrieve information from them
- Write reusable modules for ASP.NET Core
- Deploy ASP.NET Core to other environments

Leave a review - let other readers know what you think

Please share your thoughts on this book with others by leaving a review on the site that you bought it from. If you purchased the book from Amazon, please leave us an honest review on this book's Amazon page. This is vital so that other potential readers can see and use your unbiased opinion to make purchasing decisions, we can understand what our customers think about our products, and our authors can see your feedback on the title that they have worked with Packt to create. It will only take a few minutes of your time, but is valuable to other potential customers, our authors, and Packt. Thank you!

Index

www.ingramcontent.com/pod-product-compliance
Lightning Source LLC
Chambersburg PA
CBHW080628060326
40690CB00021B/4851